"Push back the desks and get your students fully enga
that they will never forget! *Stage It* is a brilliant and thoi
that brings the magic of Shakespearean theater into the cl
with Floyd Rumohr for years, I witnessed firsthand the p:
ods had on students, igniting their love for language, litei
through drama. This step-by-step book provides well-crafted, consecutive lessons
with skill-building activities, assessments, and resources that ease students ages
9-12 into the world of acting and Shakespeare. Rumohr's approach empowers students, building their focus, engagement, teamwork, and emotional intelligence."

Maureen Dillon, Retired Teacher, *Croton-Harmon Schools, USA*

"*Stage It* stands as a meticulously crafted roadmap for our frontline educators,
illuminating the transformative power of arts education. In an ever-changing
world where the virtues of empathy, connection and resilience are paramount, this
guidebook will lead the next generation to a brighter, more empathetic future."

Jennifer Wintzer, Program Manager, *Koch Center for Family Enterprise, USA*

"*Stage It* is perhaps the most teacher and student friendly guide in print today. This
is the most practical and engaging approach to teaching younger students Shakespeare—or any literary content— that I have seen in over two decades as a drama
educator. Through this process students will build community with their peers,
learn to collaborate and compromise, deepen their knowledge and understanding of Shakespeare, gain confidence in their own innate creativity, grow reflection,
assessment, and refinement skills, and learn to stand in front of an audience with
pride and claim their space in the world. I ask you, who wouldn't want this for
their students, let alone every child?"

Jennifer Shirley, Former Stages of Learning Master Teaching Artist,
Drama Curriculum Specialist, *The Juilliard School, USA*

"*Stage It* is a transformative resource that empowers educators to make Shakespearean literature engaging and accessible to students of all ages. I highly rec-
ommend this book to any educator seeking innovative methods to enrich their
teaching and inspire their students. *Stage It* not only dispels the misconception
that Shakespeare is inaccessible to younger students but also provides invaluable
techniques that significantly enhance language acquisition and comprehension.
Its strategies integrate language and movement, fostering deep connections for
students, and employs techniques that develop a deeper understanding of Shakespearean language while empowering confidence in students to express the power
of their own voices."

André Del Valle, Head of School, *Mary McDowell Friends School, USA*

"*Stage It* is an essential tool for educators to have in their classroom. It provides a
detailed map of how to "stage" a play from beginning to end and demystifies the
notion that Shakespeare's plays have to be done in a certain classical style. Teachers are empowered to tackle a play with their students in a step-by-step method,
learning together and reflecting on the process. I have been using this framework
in classrooms all over NYC and with my current population of English Language
Learners. It transforms classrooms into real rehearsal spaces with safe boundaries,
reflection and creativity."

Albert R. I. Elias, Founder and Director, *Creative Stages NYC, llc, USA*

Stage It

Stage It provides a simple-to-follow roadmap for teachers to help students dive into the dramatic, romantic, and playful world of Shakespeare. Originating from the highly successful NYC-based arts education program, Stages of Learning, this resource enables your drama, arts, or ELA class to learn the basics of Shakespeare's language, themes, characters, introductory staging, and directing. Designed for busy teachers, *Stage It* enables you to choose your own adventure depending on time, grade level collaboration, and student interest. This professional teacher's guide has simple-to-use instructions and worksheets, such as acting tools for instruction about the plot synopsis, cast of characters, and paraphrasing; and directing tools for tips about the play and the theater-making process. Accompanying the book online are abridged versions of four of Shakespeare's well-known plays: *Hamlet*, *Henry V*, *Julius Caesar*, and *Othello*, as well as paraphrasing worksheets, a culminating performance program template, and more. *Stage It* meets or exceeds many standards-based frameworks, including New York State Learning Standards in the Arts, benchmarks of the New York City Blueprint for Teaching and Learning in the Arts K-12: Theater, the U.S. Common Core/State Standards, and National Arts Standards. Teachers of students aged 9–12, as well as educators in after-school or community programs, can foster a deep connection to the material through a gradual process that engages everyone in the classroom. This approach not only brings Shakespeare's timeless stories to life but also cultivates essential skills like public speaking, teamwork, and self-expression for students of all identities.

For more information on Floyd Rumohr and the book, visit www.stage-itplays.com.

Floyd Rumohr is the founder of Stages of Learning, a nonprofit organization upon which *Stage It* is based. He is a former master teaching artist for dozens of schools, has directed several plays off-Broadway, was an Adjunct Professor of Education at the Long Island University Graduate School of Education, and has consulted on the NYC Department of Education's Blueprint for Teaching and Learning in the Arts Theater Grades PreK-12. As Associate Education Director for Theatre for A New Audience, he focused on bringing world-class Shakespeare programs to urban youth.

Also Available from Routledge Eye on Education

(www.routledge.com/eyeoneducation)

Shakespeare Amazes in the Classroom: Exploring the Bard with Gifted Students, Grades 4–8
Jennifer Szwaya

The Participatory Creativity Guide for Educators
Edward P. Clapp and Julie Rains

Learning Through Movement in the K-6 Classroom: Integrating Theatre and Dance to Achieve Educational Equity
Kell Mancini Becker

Do Your Lessons Love Your Students? Creative Education for Social Change
Mariah Rankine-Landers and Jessa Brie Moreno

Enlivening Instruction with Drama and Improv: A Guide for Second Language and World Language Teachers
Melisa Cahnmann-Taylor and Kathleen R. McGovern

Drama for the Inclusive Classroom: Activities to Support Curriculum and Social-Emotional Learning
Sally Bailey

Battling Boredom, Part 1: 99 Strategies to Spark Student Engagement
Bryan Harris

Acting it Out: Using Drama in the Classroom to Improve Student Engagement, Reading, and Critical Thinking
Juliet Hart, Mark Onuscheck, and Mary T Christel

The Classes They Remember: Using Role-Plays to Bring Social Studies and English to Life
David Sherrin

Stage It

Making Shakespeare Come Alive in Schools

Floyd Rumohr

Routledge
Taylor & Francis Group

NEW YORK AND LONDON

Designed cover image: © Getty Images

First published 2025
by Routledge
605 Third Avenue, New York, NY 10158

and by Routledge
4 Park Square, Milton Park, Abingdon, Oxon, OX14 4RN

Routledge is an imprint of the Taylor & Francis Group, an informa business

ISBN: 9781032789170 (hbk)
ISBN: 9781032789149 (pbk)
ISBN: 9781003489733 (ebk)

DOI: 10.4324/9781003489733

Typeset in Palatino
by KnowledgeWorks Global Ltd.

Access the Instructor and Student Resources: www.routledge.com/9781032789149

Dedication

To my husband, Paco, who never stopped believing.

Contents

List of Figures and Tables

Chapter 2

Chapter 3

Chapter 4

Chapter 5

Chapter 6

Chapter 7

Chapter 8

Preface

Children aged 9–12½ love to act out.

If I asked you to recall your wonder years, you might conjure vivid recollections of engaging in imaginative pursuits such as wielding a makeshift sword to combat mythical dragons, transforming into Wonder Woman to thwart evildoers, or assuming the role of detective in a quest to determine the true whereabouts of your missing hamster. From a developmental standpoint, such transcendent adventures play a crucial role in fostering the well-being of children. These experiences instill a profound sense of trust, eliciting reciprocal cooperation from the child, thereby contributing to their overall growth and development.

Stage It takes the position that if children love to act, why not give them great literature to do it? In a flash, students can embody the King in *Henry V*, a deceived general in *Othello*, an avenging prince in *Hamlet*, or a calculating murderer in *Julius Caesar*, among the dozens of other characters just waiting in the wings for your students to bring to life in each of these four plays.

In fact, using acting to bring literature to life was a wildly successful pedagogy field-tested with about 40,000 students at this age across a sixteen-year period at a New York City-based arts education organization that I founded and ran from 1994 to 2010. The approach was so successful that PS 6 Principal, Dan Feigelson (now a highly respected international literacy coach), said at the time, "I sat in on one rehearsal every week and consistently saw 100% engagement from students who I know struggle in the classroom". While Shakespeare is the literary content area for this book, the pedagogical approach can be used with any story or book to stunning results.

Over the years, schooling has become obsessed with prioritizing what is deemed "essential", often sidelining the factors that genuinely inspire, engage, and motivate children regardless of what works pedagogically. Unfortunately, theater has been scraped from the curriculum, especially in public school environments and in the earlier grades. Recognizing this gap, *Stage It* was created for classroom teachers to restore enriching learning experiences and adventures. By appealing to children as natural-born actors, *Stage It* reintegrates instruction in the art of theater as a fundamental component of their learning, development, and well-being.

Engaging in a school play transcends the mere teaching of new vocabulary or pleasing parents. You are providing a space in which students will experience a profound sense of belonging, trust, and cooperation. Through this theatrical experience, students forge meaningful connections with themselves and their peers; and gain a profound understanding of their own emotions and those of the characters they portray.

The play's the thing in which you will capture the conscience of your students.

Acknowledgments

To say that *Stage It* reflects decades of thinking, reflecting, practice, trial and error, research, and social enterprise would not be an exaggeration. I am deeply grateful to the following people for sharing their expertise, patience, and skill during my arts education career that began in the late 80s and continues to this day.

Jeffrey Horowitz and Dr. Linda Burson, who enabled my early arts education career at Theatre for a New Audience, and to Margie Salvante for sustaining and building on it.

Mentors and teachers in the Michael Chekhov technique: Kevin Cotter, Deirdre Hurst du Prey, Joanna Merlin, and the early actors/teachers of the Chekhov Theatre Ensemble: Michael Aronov, Julie Alexander, Fred Berman, Donna Browne, Cindi Clark, Paul Darrigo, David Deblinger, Ethan James Duff, Lori Funk, Tony Freeman, Sharon Gardner, Kalan Hilljac, Joe Hoover, Clark Jackson, Sean MacCormac, Seth Michael May, Jonah Mendelsohn, Julie Pasqual, Joe Ragno, Philip Levy, Jon Shaver, Melissa Schlachtmeyer, William Steel, Warren Watson, Anthony Williams, and Guy Hobson.

Stage It would not be possible without my sixteen years at Stages of Learning. Among distinctive contributions include Jessica Balboni, T. Scott Lilly, and Andrea Seigel, who helped to shape what we were doing and how we were doing it. Gratitude to the following teaching artists: Albert Iturregui-Elias, Russell Feder, Laura Frenzer, Amanda Hunt, and Claire Marie Mannle. Additional teaching artists who contributed to my thinking and immeasurably to this book include T. Scott Lilly, Andrea Seigel, Jennifer Shirley, Elizabeth Turkel, Ann Vieira, and Jennifer Wintzer.

Although April Cantor was not on staff when I began to synthesize the work into *Stage It*, her early influence on my thinking continues to resonate, and I am forever grateful for what she has taught me. Thanks also to Mike Halverson, Megan Halpern, Max Evjen, Kelly Ellenwood, Karrie Myers, Tim Parsaca, Abigail Ramsay, Sara Wood-Madera, and to early lifecycle board members Jason Lilien, Michelle Barbeau Noguchi, Peter Allen, and Michelle DiSabato. I am forever grateful for their wisdom and patience during my early career as an institutional leader with so much to learn. Much gratitude to Niko Elmaleh, board chair, Lauren Howard DePalo, vice president, and Julie Jensen for sustained governance and to the following for their service and support of Stages of Learning: Steven Bluestone, Thomas Brown, Reginald

Chambers, Sherri Cohen, Toby Fischer, Wayne Gore, Beth Ellen Keyes, George King IV, Lisa Jahns, Roberta Kirshbaum, Smita Kothuri, Karen Lack, Todd Lehman, Michael Leibowitz, Honri Marcel, Nora Peck, Mary O'Keeffe, Dawn Palo, Mark Rogers, Bruce Van Horn, and Bill Walters.

From 1994 to 2009, Stages of Learning reached approximately 40,000 students with the help of forty-two institutional funders. Much gratitude to James Jensen and Kim Tanner of the Jenesis Group for sustained leadership support and for helping me to understand that social entrepreneurs come in many forms; to Jane Barnet of the David L. Klein, Jr. Foundation for sustaining program support through good times and bad.

Gratitude is also extended to the following government, foundation, and corporate funders that invested in activities of Stages of Learning, the Chekhov Theatre Ensemble, or both: Arnhold Foundation, Arthur M. Blank Foundation, Axe-Houghton Foundation, Bay and Paul Foundations, Booth Ferris Foundation, Carefree Trust for Children, Dr. Bronner's Family Foundation, Emma A. Shaefer Charitable Trust, Howard Family Philanthropic Fund, Ira Resnick Foundation, Fribourg Family Foundation, Councilmember Dan Garodnick, Glickenhaus Foundation, JP Morgan Charitable Trust, NYC Department of Cultural Affairs, Laura Pels Foundation, Roy R. and Marie S. Neuberger Foundation, William Talbot Hillman Foundation, New York Community Trust, New York State Council on the Arts, National Endowment for the Arts, David L. Klein Foundation, One World Fund, Robert Sterling Clark Foundation, Sunny and Abe Rosenberg Foundation, Alliance Capital Management, Philip Morris Companies, Kraft Foods of North America, ConEd, Fleet Bank, Syms Corporation, Brooklyn Union Gas Company, Time Warner, 42nd Street Development Corporation, Colgate-Palmolive, Independence Community Foundation, UBS Financial Services, Weston Capital Management, and Whitman Development Company.

Classroom teachers Dr. Janet Farnham and Maureen Dillon of the Carrie E. Tompkins Elementary School for their good advice about Shakespeare for students in general and this book in particular. To teachers, administrators, and students at the following schools where I was a teaching artist between 1994 and 2004: Brooklyn: PS94, PS145, East New York Family Academy; Manhattan: PS6, PS7; Bronx: CES42, CES53, MS206B; Staten Island: PS52; New York State: Carrie E. Tomkins Elementary, Ridge Street School, Murray Avenue School; Philadelphia: Bache-Martin Elementary School; Fort Myers, Florida: Royal Palm High School, Fort Myers High School, P.L. Dunbar Middle School, Academy High School, and North Fort Myers High School.

The committed educators who served on the PS145/Stages of Learning Assessment Team (2001–2004) and have not already been mentioned include Maria Balducci, Vince Carannande, Julie Castellano, André Del Valle, Jr.,

Rosa Escóto, Rachel Fermin, Fermin Henderson, Katie Musselwhite, Michael O'Neill, Yvette Roman, Elena Marerro, Tony Mosca, Ray Torrellas, and Kristine Watts. Special thanks to Jane Remer for stewardship of the research study that helped determine what worked and what didn't for students ages 9–12.

Members of the broader arts and arts education community who contributed to my thinking through the years: Phil Alexander, Eric Booth, Gary Dayton, Carol Fineberg, Tina Grotzer, Paul King, Ginny Louloudes, Micki Hobson, Nello McDaniel, David O'Fallon, Scott Shuler, George Thorn, and Robert Zukerman. To the staff of ArtsConnection, some of whom continue to provide insights to this day: Joanna Hefferen, Carol Morgan, Carol Rice, Steve Tennen, and Rachel Watts.

Special thanks to Flloyd Kennedy, Abby Remer, and Andrew Altman for their help with some of the theater lesson plans of Chapter 5. Mrs. Plutchik provided excellent guidance on basic emotions based on Dr. Robert Plutchik's research; to Usha Goswami and Jack Hassard for their thoughts about metacognition, asking questions, and analogical reasoning in Chapter 8. Lisa Martin-Hansen at Georgia State University pointed me in a couple of very good directions; Nick Jaffe clarified some points as we prepared a version of Chapter 8 for the *Teaching Artist Journal*.

Geoffrey "Ba" and Josette Luvmour have forgotten more than I will ever know about human development. Chapter 2 would not have been possible without their collaborative insights, wisdom, and meticulous editing. Their contributions were significant and continue to shape my thinking today.

Sam Graber, whose courageous commitment and vision for the project were as graceful as they were supportive when he first intended to publish it in 2007 as a title of Accompany Publishing.

Dru DeSantis and Samantha Skarin from DeSantis Breindel for their excellent work on marketing concepts and name research; to nearly thirty classroom teachers and arts educators who participated in July 2010 focus groups that resulted in the moniker, *Stage It*.

Beloved literary agent, Manie Barron, never lacked enthusiasm for the project until his passing in January 2011. He would be happy to see it "out there".

Stephen Rainforth, graphic and web designer supreme, and Judith Rumohr, editor of remarkable stamina, without whom the wonderful world of the earlier self-published versions would likely have remained encoded on my hard drive.

Julia Dolinger, Commissioning Editor; Sofia Cohen, Editorial Assistant, from Routledge/Taylor & Francis; and Stefani Roth, advisor and dear friend whose passion for the project equaled and often excelled my own. Ian Dale and his agent, Lisa Pomerantz, for illustrations that bring the acting lesson plans of Chapter 5 to life.

It would be remiss of me were I to not mention my high school drama club leaders, Shirley Swan and Ed Paciorek, both of whom initiated me into this remarkable art form of acting.

And lastly, to Paco Arroyo, my life partner, who helped me understand that Shakespeare is as he is to me: an enduring gift.

Thank you, one and all!

Meet the Author

Floyd Rumohr is the founder of Stages of Learning (1994–2010), a nonprofit organization upon which *Stage It* is based and described by Mayor Michael Bloomberg as "one of New York City's most effective arts education programs". He is a former master teaching artist for dozens of schools, has directed several plays off- and off-off-Broadway, was an adjunct professor of education at the Long Island University Graduate School of Education, and has consulted on the NYC Department of Education's Blueprint for Teaching and Learning in the Arts Theater Grades PreK-12. As an associate education director for Theatre for A New Audience, he focused on bringing world-class Shakespeare programs to urban youth. Floyd was the first among his peers to receive a university merit fellowship in the M.F.A. acting program of Temple University and received a B.F.A. in theater from Wayne State University with several merit scholarships.

Online Instructor and Student Resources

Additional resources can be accessed online by visiting this book's product page on our website: www.routledge.com/www.routledge.com/9781032789149 then follow the links indicating Instructor and Student Resources, which you can then download directly.

- ◆ Staging Hamlet
  - – Student Paraphrasing Worksheet – Hamlet
- ◆ Staging Henry V
  - – Student Paraphrasing Worksheet – Henry V
- ◆ Staging Julius Caesar
  - – Student Paraphrasing Worksheet – Julius Caesar
- ◆ Staging Othello
  - – Student Paraphrasing Worksheet – Othello
- ◆ Culminating Performance Audience Program Template
- ◆ Shakespeare Certificate

For more information on Floyd Rumohr and the book, visit www.stageit-plays.com

1

Introduction

What I Have Witnessed and Why I Wrote This Book

Across nearly two decades in the classroom, I witnessed students vibrate with enthusiasm while acting and rehearsing. I have seen otherwise disengaged students, some described as having special needs, interpret their characters in ways that made me rethink my understanding of these classic texts. I have seen parents weep while experiencing their child's performance, whispering to me, "My son is always in trouble, and no one ever says a good word about him". My response as I nodded toward her center-stage son was, "In my class, your son was exemplary. On stage, he is sublime".

According to the NYC Department of Education Arts in Schools Report 2020–2021, theater instruction in middle schools has been declining since the

DOI: 10.4324/9781003489733-1

2016–2017 school year. Specifically, there was a 16% decrease from 59% in 2016 to 43% in 2021 of schools offering theater instruction (75% of schools responded to their survey).[1] To further compound the challenge, there is a dearth of recent research. Even the latest arts education data from the Americans for the Arts' website is for 2017.[2]

It's not much better around the world. According to the *New York Times*, "While the arts and culture space accounts for a significant amount of gross domestic product across the globe—in the United Kingdom in 2021, the arts contributed £109 billion to the economy, while in the U.S., it brought in over $1 trillion that year—arts education budgets in schools continue to get slashed. (In 2021, for instance, the spending on arts education in the U.K. came to an average of just £9.40 per pupil for the year)".[3]

I could go on and on. But I won't. It's too depressing. But you get the point: the arts have never been a priority, and this book aims to make a small contribution to changing that for the sake of our children.

What This Guide Is and Who Is It For?

This book is a resource for teachers with little to no experience in drama and a strong interest in engaging students ages 9–12½ in a forty-minute Shakespeare production (or less, depending on how much material you want to do). This book and its accompanying resources could have some use, however, for those with independent interest in Shakespeare, theater activities, the rehearsal process, and reflective practice.

Homeschoolers, parents, English language learner instructors, college professors of preservice classroom teachers, and others interested in group activities for students at this age might also benefit from the book. In this case, access to a community of at least twelve students is recommended for the acting lesson plans of Chapter 5 and to ensure there are enough students for a culminating performance described in Chapter 7.

Cluster drama teachers, teaching artists, community arts organizations, and others with theater experience are not likely to derive much new information here, except to say that the reflective practice described in Chapter 8 might provide some insights.

Regardless of the role you play in students' lives, this book will be useful if you have ever had any of the following questions:

◆ Why is acting developmentally appropriate for students aged 9–12½?
◆ How can I engage all my students in playmaking?

- ◆ How do I make the most out of the four abridged Shakespeare plays available for download?
- ◆ What are appropriate theater and Shakespearean vocabulary words?
- ◆ How do I build understanding of Shakespeare for students when I know little about him, his plays, or putting on a play?
- ◆ What are some basic theater skills and activities for students?
- ◆ How many rehearsals are needed to produce a forty-minute production with students?
- ◆ What does a director do?
- ◆ How do I notate stage movement?
- ◆ How do I facilitate a rehearsal process when I've never directed anything before?
- ◆ What is a framework for thinking about a culminating performance of a school play without costumes, lighting, sound effects, or other production values?
- ◆ How do I integrate reflective practice and inquiry into the process of playmaking?

This book can help answer these questions. It is the synthesis of field-tested tools, principles, and practices of a New York City-based nonprofit organization that partnered with public schools across a sixteen-year period and is based on research conducted at a Brooklyn elementary school described later in this chapter.

What This Guide Is Not

This book aims to provide educators with a basic framework for thinking about playmaking with limited to no resources other than a strong will to make it happen.

This book is not going to answer all your questions about theater, Shakespeare, or the English language. It focuses on information essential for an elementary or middle school teacher, or a cluster of teachers across a whole grade, to direct students in an abridged Shakespeare production. *Theater Games for the Classroom* by Viola Spolin is a classic text on theater activities for students and a highly recommended companion to this book.

This book does not provide information about how to build sets, construct costumes, design lighting effects, or any other production element. Tips for dealing with rudimentary production values are touched upon in Chapter 6, which focuses on what is realistic given existing time pressures in the classroom. A guiding principle of this book is that teachers already have a lot on their plates, and the focus should be on acting for developmental reasons described in Chapter 2.

Finally, this book does not replace professional development, coursework, or other resources that build an understanding of theater production and the capacity for it in the educational environment in which you work.

You Can Do This!

Perfectionism, no matter how well intended, could paralyze positive action if we become fixated on it. This same idea is true about the works of William Shakespeare. We shouldn't let our concept of his genius, or doing it "correctly", get in the way of doing the good thing of studying and performing his plays, no matter how imperfect we or the process might be.

Shakespeare wrote great stories about kings, queens, generals, and plotting villains – characters students love to play. He wrote about broken hearts, heroism in battle, melancholy princes, and corrupt politicians. His stories endure because we love to hear them. Just as with music, each time we hear one of his plays, we feel something, we hear something, or we learn something new because he challenges us to look at ourselves: our beauty, biases, ugliness, failures, insecurities, joys, passions, and conceits. We might laugh, cry, drop our jaws in disgust, or scratch our heads in bewilderment. Indeed, we are affected every time we engage with his words.

Students, too, can connect in meaningful ways if they have the opportunity. Such was the case at PS94, Brooklyn. A 3rd-grade student asked when rehearsing a scene from *King Lear* if she, as King Lear, could throw a red fabric into the sky because his heart was breaking. An 8-year-old girl who had no preconceived notions about Shakespeare made a father's loss of his beloved daughter palpable. She didn't know much about Shakespeare or his

> **Teaching Tip!**
>
> I have acted in, directed, and taught Shakespeare's plays for various audiences. With each new context, it felt as if I had forgotten everything I thought I knew, even though I had extensively researched the plays. I had to look up words and rethink an earlier interpretation, and I would even scratch my head after re-reading a line of dialogue that I thought I understood!
>
> Don't let a fear of "being wrong" deter you. Theatermaking is not about being "right". It's about embodying the interpretations of you and your students. It's about giving them a developmentally appropriate space to explore their ideas. And yours!

genius, so she wasn't afraid of him. She only knew what she knew: that King Lear's heart was breaking, and she wanted to find a way to convey that understanding to an audience.

Shakespeare is a gift to the world, and you can share this gift by studying and performing his plays. Don't focus on what you don't know. Discover the text along with your students to find out what might be there: in the words, in your students, and in you!

History of Stage It

The principles and practices of this book have been in the works since the mid-1980s, when I first began experimenting with many of the ideas presented here. Those ideas became institutionalized through Stages of Learning, a New York City-based nonprofit arts education organization founded by me in 1994. It existed until 2010, when the great recession earned its name and the organization dissolved. Its primary purpose involved partnerships between classroom teachers and teaching artists who collaborated on playmaking activities that culminated in performances as short as five minutes and as long as fifty, depending on educational aims and resources.

With funding from the Center for Arts Education, Empire State Partnerships/New York State Council on the Arts, and forty additional institutional funders described in "Acknowledgements", the organization provided collaborative drama instruction to about 3,000 students annually. This book synthesizes the best and most transferrable of this work.

While Stages of Learning relied on a collaborative process between teaching artists and classroom teachers, this book is intended for use by a singular teacher (or a cluster of teachers across a whole grade) with limited resources and little to no experience in theater. The underlying assumption is that resources for drama instruction are scarce to nonexistent in most schools. It is offered as a low-cost solution where even a teaching artist residency is out of the question.

This book is a bit of an experiment. Just like Stages of Learning was. Perhaps the leading research question might be, *To what degree can a classroom teacher, homeschooler, or other instructional leader or a cluster of teachers across a whole grade facilitate an abridged production of a Shakespeare play in their school or community with limited resources?* I, for one, can't wait to find out.

The Stages of Learning experiment was ongoing for sixteen years. To understand how this book came to be and, in fact, to appreciate the theories underlying its practices, it will be necessary to know more about the organizational development of Stages of Learning.

Let's start at the beginning with Michael Chekhov, whose work I was fortunate to encounter as a first-year graduate student at Temple University in 1985 and whose principles of a physical, character-based approach[4] to acting influenced my thinking. My teacher, Kevin Cotter, had such a profound impact on me that I began immediately to apply the work. Within only two weeks, I was spellbound by its effectiveness and a bit awed by its ease, having previously been subject only to the internal sufferings of the method actor. I wondered why I had never heard of a "psycho-physical"[5] approach before. By 1988, I had applied the technique to critical acclaim in several Philadelphia performances, which resulted in a few requests by my peers to teach them. With more experience as a practitioner than a teacher, I wasn't quite sure how to go about it, though I thought I might as well give it a try. My handful of students at that time evolved into a six-month waiting list by the time I arrived in New York City in 1990. Their confidence in me provided opportunities to improve my teaching and test some of my ideas. I began to move away from acting and toward other questions that would dominate my thinking.

As demand for private coaching increased beyond capacity, I struggled with a central question: *What am I training these artists to do?* Having recently graduated from a world-class conservatory program and landed an agent who was primarily focused on television in the New York market, I realized that my best years in the theater could quite possibly be behind me. I wasn't a good enough singer or dancer for Broadway, and the handful of classical theater companies in New York paid very little, if anything at all. So was I to spend my late twenties doing commercials for Chevrolet, which paid more for two days of work than I made in an entire year in the theater?

I struggled with this idea. Was I to "train" actors very much the way I was trained, which ultimately constituted overkill given that they didn't need that level of training to do commercials or daytime TV? What was I training them for? To be unemployed? To wait tables? After a time, I found it difficult to take their money when I knew they were struggling to survive.

Some of my more ambitious students approached me about forming an ensemble. This sounded like a good idea, but I was not so sure that New York City needed yet another new theater among the three hundred and fifty that already existed off and off-off-Broadway. Our emphasis on the work of Michael Chekhov would certainly distinguish us, but I wasn't convinced that that would be enough.

After some discussion among the actors, drawing upon my six years of experience at Theatre For A New Audience, and turning to Mr. Chekhov's suggestion that the creative spirit grows stronger within us when we do things for others without a "selfish note in it", we decided to offer teaching artist residencies to three New York City Public Schools free of charge. Students needed drama teachers, and actors needed jobs: it seemed like a great match. It was 1994: The Chekhov Theatre Ensemble and the Stages of Learning program were born.

Following professional development to enhance teaching skills, the actors visited the schools to teach drama and the literature curriculum[6] in partnership with public school teachers once each week for several weeks. While we knew that acting worked with kids, especially aged 9–12½, we didn't know why and we also knew that certain aspects of theater-making didn't work at all. We had more questions than answers and sought to inquire into essential questions. With leadership funding from the Center for Arts Education, New York State Council on the Arts, The Jenesis Group, and Niko Elmaleh, Stages of Learning Board Chairman, we sought to clarify elements necessary for success.

Between 2001 and 2004, we used a collaborative action research and assessment (CARA) approach during a four-year study at PS145, Brooklyn. Facilitated by nationally known researcher, Jane Remer, the CARA process uses a mixed methods approach to the collection, analysis, synthesis, and interpretation of data. The study, which engaged classroom teachers, administrators, and teaching artists in action research, focused on the following lines of inquiry:

YEAR ONE
Inquiry:
What is essential to our art form?
What of that is developmentally appropriate for children?

YEAR TWO
Inquiry:
How do we translate artistic principles into 'kid-friendly' practices?

YEAR THREE
Inquiry:
What is a developmentally appropriate scope and sequence of instructional activity for children grades 3-7 in collaborative public school contexts?

YEAR FOUR
Inquiry:
What is scalable in multiple contexts?

The study ultimately found that:

◆ Students improved work habits, habits of mind, and skills and performance experience that demonstrated their understanding of the literature (Shakespeare).

◆ Students developed no less than a mastery of 16th-century English of the scenes upon which they worked.

◆ Students paraphrased tales and themes of *Macbeth*, *Romeo and Juliet*, *Midsummer Night's Dream*, and *Hamlet* into stories that make sense in their own lives and shared these understandings with their peers and parents.

◆ Students learned and then improved their performance skills, such as staccato and legato movement; made small contracting shapes, big expanding shapes, and smooth transitions between movements; and demonstrated beginning, middle, and end in their stage movements.

◆ Students learned to make theatrical choices for creating their choral characters as they learned to stand, walk, and speak like their character (archetype); moved in space with a clear sense of direction and confidence; expressed meaning and intention when saying their character's lines; and radiated energy as they focused their character's thoughts and feelings.

◆ Students demonstrated, wrote, and talked about the play; they were able to relate the story of the play, the characters they played, and the play's meaning to themselves in their young American lives. They made connections by analogy and comparison and found echoes of the story in their home and school situations.

Following the study, Jane Remer continued to play a leadership role in assessment as chair of the Assessment Steering Committee from 2004 to 2007, which examined ways in which the above information could inform Stages of Learning practices.

Through those and subsequent years, Stages of Learning evolved into a respected drama program, having been recognized by Mayor Michael Bloomberg as one of the most effective arts education organizations serving the city. In 2009, the program was adopted by Queens Theatre in the Park (now Queens Theatre) to stabilize the program in an intensely competitive environment for smaller nonprofits struggling to compete for contracting resources. The recession earned its "greatness" during the partnership, however, as nonprofits around the country began to feel the effects. Queens Theatre, struggling with challenges unrelated to the acquisition of Stages of Learning, no longer had the capability to sustain an education program, and the Stages of

Learning board chose to separate and dissolve the organization. We believed that the environment could no longer support the quality services for which Stages of Learning had become known.

Over 40,000 students at dozens of schools, both urban and suburban, benefited from the ideas presented in the Stage It series. Indeed, the concepts have been so thoroughly tested in many different contexts that my hope is that you continue to build on them. Some things will work, and some won't. Some things might appear mundane and simplistic, and you might skip over them. And still, others might surprise you and test your assumptions and biases. It is up to you to decide what works in your classroom and for you as a learner.

The stage is set. Villains, heroes, lovers, and generals are among the cast of characters you'll find at these grade levels for your students. Your coaching, instruction, and modeling will be as Michelangelo's chisel: tools to chip away until you can see the emergent characters who live within your students and in some of the greatest stories ever told.

How to Use This Guide

While intended to be thorough, this book will answer some questions and raise others. You might find, for example, that the archetype pose described in this context might be more relevant at different points in the process than is recommended in the scope and sequence. Additionally, your students might struggle with basic concepts, such as audibility, and instruction in archetype pose or tableau vivant, for example, might have to be delayed.

Success will rely on your capacity to self-regulate and monitor your own

> **Teaching Tip!**
>
> A lesson plan about audibility is not included in this book. The reason for that is because children will often easily respond to a prompt, "Louder" while rehearsing. In addition, casting students in choral character teams will ensure that audibility will not be such a challenge as it would be if only one student were playing each character.

thinking and learning as much as it will rely on your teaching skills. This book requires a dynamic interchange between you as a teacher and as a learner.

The following sequentially describes the chapters in this book:

Chapter 1: Introduction
This chapter encourages teachers to engage in the process regardless of their experience level with his plays, specifically, or with theater in general. Topics include the decades-long history of the principles and practices described in this book.

Chapter 2: Why Acting and Why These Stage It Plays for Students Aged 9–12½?[7]

This chapter explores the major developmental themes for students at this age and why acting is so important. It synthesizes research in child development and aims to describe key developmental stages in a child's life in a way that is useful for classroom teachers, teaching artists, and others who interact with students. Themes of justice, fairness, honesty, trust, and adventure are described, along with some classroom strategies that represent them. A brief discussion about why *Hamlet, Henry V, Othello,* and *Julius Caesar* were chosen for the Stage It series is also included.

Chapter 3: Shakespeare Basics

Why do Shakespeare? Are his plays relevant for students at this age? Thee, thou, and wherefore: what's with all the pronoun madness? If you have questions like that, then this chapter will help answer them. In addition, vocabulary coined by Shakespeare that might be used on a word wall and fun facts about acting troupes in Shakespeare's day, gender, learning lines, and cue scripts are discussed. Perhaps you might form a Shakespeare troupe of your own?

Chapter 4: Scope and Sequence

Let's start at the very beginning! This chapter describes the scope and sequence of acting lessons and activities parallel to the rehearsal process for either (1) one teacher doing all five acts or (2) one teacher doing one Act. It's up to you how much material to stage.

Chapter 5: Acting Lesson Plans

These long-form, field-tested lesson plans with embedded assessments and sample reflection questions provide the basic skills for students to stage as much of the play as you, and they, decide upon. Staccato/legato movement and speech, archetype pose, tableau vivant, emotional expression, and focal point are among the concepts students should know, understand, and be able to do.

Chapter 6: The Rehearsal Process

"3, 2, 1 – ACTION!" It's not about perfection. It's about practice! Rehearsal is a cyclical process of practice, feedback, and more practice. Want to know what "blocking" is and how to do it? This is the chapter for you! It contains practical advice about noting stage directions/movement, a task that could also be assigned to a student or team of students with emerging management skills.

Chapter 7: The Culminating Performance

It's show time! Performance of some kind is integral to the process of theater-making and is encouraged regardless of grade level. Focus is on the acting and costumes, props, and scenery are omitted or lightly included. Topics include identifying the audience, program outline, preparing the space, audience takeaways, and narration with Instructor and Student Resources like an audience program.

Chapter 8: Inquiry and Reflection

Albert Einstein once said, "Any fool can know. The point is to understand". Indeed, doing without understanding can result in an exhilarating experience with little to no meaning behind it. This chapter explores key concepts of asking questions and reflecting on activities to build understanding. Metacognition, kinds of reflection, relationship to assessment, what to listen for, and sample questions using *Othello* as an example are among the topics.

Chapter 9: Instructor and Student Resources

 Choose your play! There are four plays in the series: *Hamlet*, *Julius Caesar*, *Othello*, and *Henry V*. Each is available separately for download to "grab and go" without requiring additional resources to stage it. Topics for each title include interpreting the play, notable quotations, contemporary English versions as a teacher's guide, plot synopsis brimming with new vocabulary, cast of characters, acting scripts with footnotes for vocabulary, and glossary with word pronunciations for each of:

   ◆ *Staging Hamlet*

Something is rotten in the state of Denmark, but not for long! Hamlet will soon set things right. That is, if he doesn't spend too much time talking to the ghost of his murdered father. Some of the most famous quotations in the English language appear in Hamlet and they give students a lot to think about. "Brevity is the soul of wit", "To be or not to be", and "Though this be madness; yet there is method in't" are just a few. Twelve characters.

   ◆ *Staging Julius Caesar*

"Beware the ides of March" warns the soothsaying Chorus in one of Shakespeare's most famous tragedies. Will Julius Caesar discover the conspirators who plotted his demise before the dreaded date of March 15? What dreaded fate awaits Caesar in the senate chamber? Friendship, betrayal, and murder take center stage in this classic story. Ten characters.

◆ *Staging Othello*

The classic tale of jealousy – the green-eyed monster that devours Othello's soul! Othello, a general in the army, loves his wife, Desdemona, "not wisely, but too well". The villainous Iago manipulates Othello into believing that Desdemona has a boyfriend on the side. Othello's jealousy and mistrust lead to a tragic conclusion that reveals a terrible truth. Nine characters.

◆ *Staging Henry V*

"Once more unto the breach dear friends, once more!" we hear before the great battle of Agincourt. Beware! Conspiratorial snakes hide in the grass waiting to strike and undermine our beloved king. Will King Henry and his "band of brothers" defeat the French in battle and assume the throne? Will he marry the French Princess? Not even a muse of fire can answer those questions. Stage it to find out! Twenty-one characters.

Each of the above plays includes details about how and when to use the various resources in each book. Additional resources for each play include Shakespeare certificates, culminating activity program template, and student paraphrasing worksheets.

Notes

1 *Arts in Schools Report 2020–2021*. NYC Department of Education. P11, 15.
2 "Americans for the Arts Research Reports Arts Education". https://www.americansforthearts.org/by-program/reports-and-data/research-studies-publications/americans-for-the-arts-publications/research-reports#education. February 20, 2024.
3 Brownell, Ginanne. "The Mind-Expanding Value of Arts Education". *New York Times*. May 2, 2023.
4 Michael Chekhov is known as the "acting genius" of the 20th century in Russia largely because of his ability to convincingly play a wide range of

different characters. While there are many other acting techniques used by professional actors, the principles of Michael Chekhov focus on the body and character and are among the most developmentally appropriate for children ages 9–12½. Chekhov had two major influences: Constantin Stanislavski of the Moscow Art Theater and Rudolf Steiner, father of Waldorf Education.

5 Michael Chekhov's work was predicated on the idea that the mind, body, soul, and emotions are inextricably linked.

6 While Shakespeare is the focus of Stage It, Shakespeare was among several authors available for the school play, most of whom involved the reading curriculum. Teaching artists would adapt books students were already reading into a school play, similarly to how Stage It has adapted some of Shakespeare's plays.

7 Students approaching 13 years of age responded better to solo acting opportunities than to choral character teams (in which several students played the same part) in Stages of Learning classrooms. The methods presented here could work with 13-year-olds though focusing on solo acting opportunities with intermittent choral passages are likely to be the most successful.

2

Why Acting and Why These Stage It Plays for Students Aged 9–12½?[1]

Why Is Acting Essential for Students Aged 9 through 12½?

In the developmental ages between 9 and 12½ years old, children exhibit a profound affinity for the performing arts as a means of learning and expressing their emotions. This age group specifically gravitates toward various artistic forms, including acting, singing, dancing, and even the occasional magic show.

Parents with children within these age ranges could potentially find themselves in attendance at dozens of performances of one kind or another, ranging

DOI: 10.4324/9781003489733-2

from school productions to impromptu shows in the backyard, basement, street, or wherever else the child's imagination takes them. This engagement with the performing arts not only provides a platform for self-expression but also contributes significantly to the holistic development of the child during these formative years.

Children ages 9 through 12½ exhibit a natural inclination toward acting, a phenomenon recognized by developmental expert Geoffrey "Ba" Luvmour, who holds an MA in Psychology and is internationally acclaimed for his expertise in whole-family experiential learning. Luvmour identifies a significant shift in children's consciousness that occurs around the age of 9 when they grapple with the awareness of personal mortality. This pivotal realization marks a transformative phase in the child's self-awareness and understanding of their world.

Comparing 7, 8-year-olds with 9, 10-year-olds, Alison Giovanelli et al. "explains how in comparison to the younger children who do recognize and understand emotions, the older children understand more about the complexity of emotions and are more sensitive to moral and social codes related to empathic behaviors".[2]

Consequently, drama emerges as a crucial avenue for their cognitive and emotional development during this period. One outcome of this shift is that dramatic expression can contribute positively to the comprehensive growth and well-rounded development of children in this age group.

So what exactly changes as the child grows? According to the Wallace Foundation, "As children move through the elementary grades (ages 7–10), they have an increased need for more complex cognitive skills like planning, organizing, and goal setting, as well as empathy, social awareness, and perspective taking. In late elementary school, many children shift toward an emphasis on more specific interpersonal skills, such as the capacity to develop sophisticated friendships, engage in prosocial and ethical behavior, and resolve conflicts".[3]

As a child matures, significant shifts occur in their perception and interaction with the world – their field of knowing changes. Prior to reaching 8 years of age, a child is primarily egocentric, perceiving themselves as the center of the world and the world as an extension of their own body. Their worldview is characterized by a self-centric understanding – for instance, attributing *The chair bumps into me because I am at the center of the world*, kind of thing. *I didn't bump into the chair.* The child before 8 years of age doesn't conceptualize themselves as the one in motion; rather, they perceive the chair as magical and moving toward them.

Before the age of 8, a child predominately interacts with the world through sensory explorations and experiences. Considerations for empathy or interest in social dynamics have not yet emerged. Children are inclined to seek pleasant sensory experiences and avoid unpleasant ones. Consequently, the ability to step into the emotions of another, a vital skill in acting, is generally beyond the developmental capacities of most 8-year-olds. Understanding these developmental nuances is crucial for effective theater-making and for fostering a comprehensive understanding of children's psycho-emotional evolution.

At about 9 years of age, children experience a profound shift in awareness regarding personal mortality that significantly impacts their worldview. Death defines a relationship. This newfound awareness of death reshapes their understanding of relationships, as death becomes a defining aspect of human connection. Alongside awareness of mortality, children begin to comprehend the cycles of nature and life, and the vastness of the world around them. This transition marks a departure from the self-centered perspective of earlier years, as they become increasingly attuned to the broader realities of existence. With awareness of mortality at 9 years of age, children develop a yearning for interpersonal connection characterized by empathy, honesty, and a sense of justice. They seek meaningful relationships where they can both give and receive care, and they crave opportunities for adventure and exploration. Ultimately, this emerging awareness prompts a desire for deeper, more relational forms of love as they navigate their evolving understanding of the world and their place within it.

Collaborative for Academic Social and Emotional Learning (CASEL) describes five areas of "Caring School Communities" that could help build interpersonal connections while navigating the complex world noted above. Such communities:

◆ Build caring relationships with and among students
◆ Directly teach social skills
◆ Create calm, orderly learning environments through the effective use of classroom management practices[4]
◆ Help students acquire self-discipline through a caring and effective approach to discipline[5]

Navigating the intricate world of emotions even in caring communities can be both frightening, mysterious, and captivating for children aged 9 through 12½ years old. How can they decipher their feelings and the feelings of others? How can they learn to trust themselves and others? How can they master the interpersonal and social world and engage in relationships that ensure optimal well-being? Learning to trust themselves and others, while mastering interpersonal and social dynamics, emerges as a critical imperative for their well-being.

What better way than acting to facilitate these developmental milestones? Through acting, children can safely immerse themselves in the emotions and feelings of the characters they play. By embodying different emotional states, students gain firsthand experience and understanding of feelings, learning to identify them and their appropriate names. This is fear; that is sadness. This is joy; that is disgust. And so on. This process effectively equips children with the vocabulary of emotions, which is fundamental to acting.

At this developmental stage, emotions play a vital role in children's comprehension of themselves and the world around them, mirroring the role of emotions play for actors in the context of working on a character. Consequently, the relationship between children and the adults in their lives is of critical importance. It is a characteristic of the age that the student seeks guidance from trusted mentors to navigate the complexities of emotions and interpersonal relationships. Directors, teachers, and other supportive adults who encourage the child to explore a spectrum of feelings contribute to fostering optimal trust and facilitating social development.

Trust flourishes as children engage in experiential learning encompassing honesty, justice, fairness, and adventure (see Table 2.3). Acting serves as an adventurous journey in itself, immersing participants in the complex realm of feelings and interpersonal relationships. Embedded in *Hamlet, Henry V, Othello, Romeo and Juliet*, and other plays are differing perspectives on these themes.

Engaging in character portrayal through acting cultivates various intelligences as students learn self-trust and collaboration among classmates. Control or mastery of bodily movements is necessary for effective acting, leading to the development of bodily-kinesthetic skills and then mastery. Additionally, spatial awareness is honed as students navigate placement and stage blocking.

In theater, two significant intelligences come into play: intrapersonal and interpersonal. Intrapersonal intelligence, which is the capacity to know oneself, is vividly realized through acting. Portraying diverse characters prompts actors to explore various facets of their own identity, fostering self-awareness through introspection and self-reflection. The self-reflective process enhances acting skills, leads to sophisticated acting, deepens appreciation of the play, and promotes greater self-knowledge (see Chapter 8).

Interpersonal skills develop through interaction with fellow student actors, the teacher as director of the play, and the audience. Students thrive on understanding and embodying the intricacies and subtleties of the emotions of their characters, refining their ability to navigate subtle emotional nuances. Interacting with the other students as they play their characters further enriches their interpersonal experiences.

Under the guidance of a skillful classroom teacher and through meaningful theatrical experiences, acting brings forth the best in children. Embracing the adventure of embodying their characters, receiving guidance from supportive adults, and collaboratively working toward a culminating performance fosters growth and encourages students to actively engage in the world around them.

See Table 2.1 by Ba Luvmour, Table 2.2,[6] and Table 2.3.

> **Teaching Tip!**
>
> "Field of Knowing" refers to ways in which we understand and perceive the world. Our field of knowing shapes our worldview, influencing how we organize our experiences and relationships. It is an inherent aspect of ourselves, guiding our interactions and understanding throughout life. Understanding a child's field of knowing offers insight into how they navigate concepts such as space, time, identity, respect, community, love, perceptions of death, gender, values, aesthetics, play, meaning-making, and natural, non-sectarian spirituality during their formative years.

Table 2.1 Intelligences Actualization[a]

"Intelligence"	Actualization
Emotional The ability to recognize, comprehend, and navigate all of our emotions, encompassing awareness and identification of emotions without succumbing to fear or avoidance.	**Engaging in acting, myth, drama, and theatrical performances** with the skill to empathize with the character's emotions and convey them authentically. This skill requires spending dedicated time with reliable mentors who can oversee, guide, and support the self-regulation and discernment of various emotions. The mentor's role is indispensable in helping the student effectively connect with and express emotions in a suitable manner. The foundation of genuine emotional intelligence is reliant on the establishment of self-trust. As empathy develops, typically between ages 8 through 12, a child gains increased awareness and compassion for the feelings of others. During this developmental period, trustworthy mentors play a pivotal role in shaping and nurturing emotional intelligence in the child.

(Continued)

Table 2.1 (Continued)

"Intelligence"	Actualization
Interpersonal The ability to make distinctions among others and oneself in relationship to others.	**Acting** and all performing arts; **safe space to explore feelings with friends and close elders; cooperating activities that emphasize values; chance to exercise fairness**, i.e., deciding chore responsibilities for all family members; full participation in class government; ecology; helping the less fortunate; conversations about death.
Intrapersonal The ability to know oneself.	**Acting; myth; support to understand personal feelings through inquiry and humor; time with trusted teenager; conversations about death; non-lecturing exploration of elder's feelings; inspirational environments, i.e., cathedrals, mountain tops, etc.**
Verbal Linguistic Awareness of the sounds, rhythms, inflections, meaning, order, and functions of words.	**Reading and listening to books and stories**, particularly inspirational ones; **acting** and all performing arts; opportunity to classify things; writing without constraint, i.e., poetry; dialogue with friends and close elders; Eurhythmy; foreign language.
Logical-Mathematical Creating and operating on strings of symbols that represent "reality".	Continuation and expansion of manipulatives, i.e., Mortensen math; continuation of home-based math in cooking, building, etc.; **cooperative learning**, i.e., rhythm games; **beginning abstractions; simple word problems**; lots of music, i.e., beginning relationship to scale, chords, and notes as well as sophisticated listening to compositions.
Musical The controlled movement of sound in time.	As much music as the child is willing to engage; lessons where appropriate but minimum pressure to perform; dance; singing; music inclusive of all time periods and cultures; some reading and notation.
Bodily-Kinesthetic Mastery over motion of the body and the ability to successfully manipulate objects.	**Cooperative play; increased skill training**; some team sports, but minimize winning and losing; **rhythmic exercises,** especially dance; nature/wilderness exploration, i.e., canoeing, **drama**; Eurhythmy; lots of free time.
Spatial The capacity to accurately perceive, transform, modify, and recreate aspects of the visual world.	Painting; drawing; building; sewing; opportunity to explore rhythms of seasons; beginning astronomy; model making; field trips to skyscrapers, caves, and the ocean; varied movement modes, i.e., horseback, bicycle, motorboat, roller skates; **sophisticated use of patterns and shapes** and blocks.

[a] Original chart created by Ba Luvmour, MA in 2006, with the latest update contributed by Josette Luvmour, PhD in 2024. Used with permission.

Table 2.2 Epistemology 0 through 18 Years: Children's Field of Knowing [a]

≈ Age 8	Age 9	Age 10	Age 11	Age 12
• Begins to engage in community activities • Readiness for new tasks with caring guidance • Learns best from accepting individuals • Developing concern for fairness and justice • Curiosity in exploring the theater arts and how things work • Values peer assessment • Relaxed in safe situations **Do:** • Create safe sensory explorations that enhance creativity and emotional expression • Establish clear boundaries • Recognize preference for sensory experiences. • Longer exposure for pleasant; shorter for unpleasant sensations • Provide opportunities to participate in modest public performances	• Thrives in trustworthy environments • Values peer assessment • Seeks guidance from trustworthy mentors • Searches for inspirational opportunities • Fairness is important • Engages in rule discussions • Prefers to work with a chosen partner • Inquisitive about nature • Learning emotional expression • Learns through stories • Shares and collaborates • Curious about death as a natural part of life **Do:** • Promote collaboration • Promote physical expression and confidence • Engage conversations about life cycles and death • Engage guided interpersonal learning • Provide opportunities to assist others	• Embraces community values • Prefers clear fair boundaries • Dedicated to fairness • Enjoys physical activity • Thrives in community and group learning • Enjoys teaching younger children • Desires emotional connection • Developing empathy • Growing conscience • Seeking inspirational experiences • Receptive to guided interpersonal learning • Able to make new friends • Willing to share leadership • Cooperative and adaptive in social situations **Do:** • Engage approaches to resolve conflict • Promote cooperative activities • Embark on Inspirational Journeys together	• Passionate about conflict resolution and relationship restoration • Learning social graces (inclusion/exclusion) • Enjoys engaging in theatrical activities • Vast appetite for social engagements • Learning to navigate the spectrum of emotions • Growing ability to understand varied perspectives • Enjoys cooperative play • Increasing skill development • Enjoys rhythmic exercises • Empathy toward animals • Seeks inspirational opportunities • Able to celebrate the success of others **Do:** • Foster a positive and supportive atmosphere • Explore rhythms in nature • Provide inspirational opportunities • Play cooperative games	• Demonstrates understanding of fairness • Growing understanding of empathy • Insightful into interpersonal dynamics • Passionate about drama and performances • Enjoys revision and practice • Appreciation for visible culminations of activities • Heightened peer values taking on importance • Well-developed emotional intelligence • Respectful of others' feelings • Trusts their own feelings – healthy self-trust • Trusts healthy mentors • Effective communication of emotions **Do:** • Engage interpersonal learning curriculum • Ba a trustworthy feeling mentor • Embark on exciting adventures with them
<Age 8 Learning primarily occurs through the orientation of the body in the environment and safe sensory explorations.				**Age 13-18** Identity explorations occur as teenagers seek to uncover and understand themselves.

[a] Created in collaboration with Josette Luvmour, PhD, and the author. Used with permission.

Table 2.3 Developmental Themes and Classroom Strategies

Theme	Definition	Classroom Strategies
Justice	The quality of being guided by truth, reason, and fairness; righteousness, equitableness, or moral rightness.	Boundaries and procedures that are reasonable and applied to all members of the classroom will help to build a just classroom environment. If a boundary is broken for any reason, engage students by asking why the boundary was broken. Procedural consistency is essential in a just classroom, such as having the Hamlet choral team present their work today and the Ophelia choral team present on the following day.
Fairness	Free from bias, dishonesty, or injustice.	Embed assessment with publicly shared criteria and indicators against which all students' performance is measured. If audibility is the criterion of the day then it applies to everyone, for example. If exploring archetype poses then hold all students accountable for remaining still on cue.
Honesty	Honorable in principles, intentions, and actions; truthful, sincere, credible, frank; free of deceit or fraud.	Adults with whom students interact most closely should model honesty in every interaction. This can be done even when not instructing students! Should a colleague come into the room for any reason, use it as an opportunity to model frankness, sincerity, and truthfulness audibly and in line of sight of students. Allow students to ask questions about lying, cheating, and speaking the truth.
Trust	Reliance on the integrity, strength, ability, and surety of a person or thing; confidence.	Model strength, integrity, and confidence for students. If you make a mistake, be frank and confident about it! Don't lie or cover it up. Let the students see how confident you can be even amid chaos, noise, and other distractions, and ask for their help. It will help build trust.
Adventure	An exciting, unusual, bold, and risky undertaking or enterprise.	Introduce activities with judicious use of excitement in the tone of your voice (if you overdo it, students' honesty and truth "antennae" will go up). When something is exciting or unusual to them, don't be afraid to express the sense of adventure. *During today's rehearsal, we will go to the fields of Agincourt for one of the most famous battles in all history!* for example.

Why These Stage It Plays?

Hamlet, Henry V, Othello, and *Julius Caesar* are included among downloadable titles in the Stage It series and are recommended for you to explore and stage with your students.

Because these plays might be lesser known for classroom use at this age group, they provide a wonderful opportunity for you to engage, learn, explore, and derive meaning together with your students. Don't worry if you are unfamiliar with the plays or haven't encountered them in the past. That's part of the idea! The Stage It series is intended to begin a learning adventure for everyone involved and enable children's interpretations to come to the fore.

The selection of these titles begs the question, *why these plays over more commonly known titles such as* Romeo and Juliet *or* Midsummer Night's Dream?

Midsummer Night's Dream and *Romeo and Juliet* have frequently been explored in Stages of Learning classroom settings, often yielding great success. The magical fairies of *Midsummer* and the poignant portrayal of teenage angst of *Romeo and Juliet* deeply resonated with students. Both plays would make excellent opportunities for staging with students, although the teenage suicides in *Romeo and Juliet* may pose sensitivities within certain school communities.[7] They are, however, among the most studied, and resources are more readily available. The more commonly known plays for this age group could foster existing assumptions and ideas rather than generate new interpretations.

Not knowing so much about the play could contribute to a process that generates new interpretations and ideas in youngsters. For instance, students at PS 6 in Manhattan interpreted Hamlet as the Avenger! I had never considered playing Hamlet from this perspective despite the Ghost asking Hamlet to, "Avenge me!" Perhaps I was asleep at the wheel. Regardless, the students taught me something new with their fresh interpretation. Chapter 5 explores the concept of archetypes in detail.

Whatever play(s) you choose, circumspection is advisable to ensure the choice is sensible and appropriate. Stage It deliberately ventured in directions that would encourage a new literary adventure for both students and teachers to embark upon together. Each of the Stage It plays also exemplifies the developmental themes of justice, fairness, honesty, trust, and adventure described above. For example:

◆ *Hamlet*: Hamlet is a justice warrior, seeking vengeance for his father's murder to restore a fair and just kingdom.

◆ *Henry V*: Conquering an enemy proves to be the adventure of a lifetime for Henry, yet perhaps it isn't as much of an adventure as marrying the French princess.

◆ *Julius Caesar*: Julius Caesar is brutally murdered in the Senate chamber. Brutus, formerly a trusted friend of Caesar, ultimately betrayed his friend by supporting the plot.

◆ *Othello*: Iago's deceit and betrayal of trust drive an otherwise loving husband to brutally murder his wife, all based on a falsehood orchestrated by the villainous Iago.

Notes

1 Students approaching 13 years of age responded better to solo acting opportunities than to choral character teams (in which several students played the same part) in Stages of Learning classrooms. The methods presented here could work with 13-year-olds, though focusing on solo acting opportunities with intermittent choral passages is likely to be the most successful.

2 Giovanelli, Alison, Christina F. Mondi, and Arthur Reynolds. "Fostering socio-emotional learning through early childhood intervention". *International Journal of Child Care and Education Policy.* 15, Article Number 6 (2021).

3 Jones, Stephanie M., Katharine E. Brush, Samantha Wettje, Thelma Ramirez, Aashna Poddar, Alisha Kannarr, Sophie P. Barnes, Annie Hooper, Gretchen Brion-Meisels, and Edwin Chng. "Navigating SEL From the Inside Out". Wallace Foundation. November 2022.

4 Rehearsals aren't always "calm" and could be described as "organized chaos" in which children's generative interpretations are explored in a safe field of knowing.

5 Collaborative Classroom. Caring School Community K-8. Retrieved online March 22, 2024. https://info.collaborativeclassroom.org/caring-school-community-k-8?utm_term=casel%20framework&utm_campaign=CSC+-+National&utm_source=adwords&utm_medium=ppc&hsa_acc=9861834821&hsa_cam=12966904783&hsa_grp=124796945474&hsa_ad=519116708557&hsa_src=g&hsa_tgt=kwd-1027273283237&hsa_kw=casel%20framework&hsa_mt=b&hsa_net=adwords&hsa_ver=3&gad_source=1&gclid=Cj0KCQjw2PSvBhDjARIsAKc2cgNSw1IhkbZ-C2l7mGI1i8qm6oyFn7P0t1hPM7Pq2Jxzq5d9MaKLucO8aAhXdEALw_wcB

6 Luvmour, 2022, pp. 3–4.

7 Othello technically completes suicide, but he is an adult, which provides some age distance that might not hit so close to home as it does in *Romeo and Juliet*.

3

Shakespeare Basics

Why Do Shakespeare?

Let's acknowledge the historical elephant in the room: William Shakespeare. He was a remarkable playwright, and some would say he was the greatest in the English language. He is indeed no longer with us, and he was a white man. However, it's essential to recognize that:

♦ **Global Significance**: Shakespeare's work transcends time and borders. No other writer in the English language has been translated

DOI: 10.4324/9781003489733-3

into as many languages or performed as frequently across the globe. His plays grace stages from public parks to prestigious theaters, and they continue to inspire reinterpretations in various art forms, including film, dance, visual arts, and new literary adaptations.

◆ **Linguistic Innovation:** Shakespeare's contribution to the English language is immeasurable. He coined and popularized around 3,000 words and phrases, enriching our vocabulary like no other writer. His writings have given us some of the most profound sayings in English literature. So much so that many people think they are quoting *Bible* scripture when they are quoting Shakespeare, as in:
  – 'Tis neither here nor there. (*Othello*)
  – Neither a borrower nor a lender be. (*Hamlet*)
  – To thine own self be true. (*Hamlet*)
  – We few, we happy few, we band of brothers. (*Henry V*)

◆ **Universal Themes:** Shakespeare's stories feature characters like kings, queens, generals, and fortune tellers that children are naturally drawn to. His tales explore universal themes such as broken hearts, triumphs in battle, gender identity, melancholy, and political corruption. These themes continue to resonate with the human experience, making his work as relevant today as it was in his era.

◆ **Emotional Resonance:** Shakespeare had a unique talent for crafting words that resonate like music. Hearing his text spoken aloud evokes powerful emotions, challenges our perceptions, and encourages introspection. Speaking his lines is akin to singing along to a favorite song, a process that children find delightful.

By embracing the abridged versions of Shakespeare's plays described in this book, you can provide students with an engaging and accessible entry point into this literary treasure trove. These adaptations (available separately for download) allow students to step onto the stage from day one, immersing themselves in the characters and their emotions, just like professional actors and directors.

Understanding and appreciation grow over time, fostering a deep connection to the material through a gradual process that engages everyone in the classroom. This approach not only brings Shakespeare's timeless stories to life but also cultivates essential skills like public speaking, teamwork, and self-expression for students of all identities and races.

By using the Stage It abridged versions of his plays in conjunction with this book, you can get students on their feet on day one to start speaking and moving right away as they explore characters and their accompanying emotions the same way professional directors and actors do. Understanding develops over time for everyone involved with an approach to staging that, day by day, builds connection through a theatrical rehearsal process that engages everyone in the classroom.

The process also helps to bridge the philosophical divide between Balanced Literacy and the Science of Reading. In addition, drama has been shown to increase students' abilities to communicate, develop higher-order group processes, and is even referenced in many standards at all grade levels in the Common Core and State standards of the U.S. In other countries, like Australia, drama is part of the curriculum, and many English Language Learning countries engage in plays to learn the language. A play has also been effective for student engagement for those who might otherwise tune out.

The stage is set: Villains, heroes, lovers, and generals are among the players. 3-2-1-ACTION!

Myth vs. Floyd's Facts

Many myths about Shakespeare have evolved. Below are some examples along with my response:

Table 3.1 Myths vs. Floyd's Facts

Myth	Floyd's Facts
"Shakespeare is elitist".	Were he alive today, Shakespeare would probably laugh at how his plays have been elevated to high art. At the very least, he would be surprised because, at the time, plays were not considered good literature. That distinction went to historians and poets. Plays were popular entertainment, more akin to Netflix or the "Housewives of New York". To illustrate the point further: If a woman attended the theater, she was generally assumed to be a prostitute. Later in his career, however, his plays were performed for the English court.
"Kids don't like Shakespeare".	That's because most kids are introduced to his plays by sitting in their chairs and reading them. The kids grow up, and they become adults who introduce kids in the same way. And the cycle continues. Shakespeare never intended for his plays to be read or analyzed in English class. Let's not forget that most of the younger apprentice actors of the time were likely illiterate and they had to learn their lines by having someone read them aloud until they could memorize them. He intended the plays to be spoken aloud and acted out.

(Continued)

Table 3.1 (Continued)

Myth	Floyd's Facts
	Try it yourself! Stand up and speak aloud a section from one of the acting scripts. Even if you don't know what it means at first, some kind of meaning will resonate: emotional, psychological, kinesthetic, and/or cognitive. Understanding will come over time as you explore the text as actors and directors do: they don't know everything either, but they endeavor to develop their own interpretations. And, trust me, the most famous actors and their directors use dictionaries and Google for words and phrases they might not know or understand. Stage It has prepared a paraphrased, line-by-line teacher's guide to help with this.
"Shakespeare is not relevant".	Really? Othello's "Green-eyed monster of jealousy" isn't relevant, as he believes in lies that result in murdering his wife? Julius Caesar's political assassination and betrayal by a good friend? King Henry and his troops charge "Once more unto the breach" as they conquer a country in what he believes is a noble war? Or, in Hamlet, a prince who seeks to avenge his murdered father for something that is, in fact, "rotten in the state of Denmark"? No other dramatist in the English language is produced as much around the world, translated into more languages, or re-interpreted into different contexts. This is why his characters, plots, and themes are as relevant today as they were when he first wrote them.
"There are too many confusing sayings in the plays".	Absolutely! "It's Greek to me!" was made famous in *Julius Caesar* and even reflects this idea. I sometimes speak the passages aloud multiple times and look up the meaning of words myself to make sense of them. But we shouldn't let a little confusion, fear, or even our own biases stop us from playing with the text. Think of it as a riddle, which can be a fun puzzle. At first, a riddle confuses, but once solved, it can be a revelation.
"I don't really know enough to teach Shakespeare - and frankly didn't enjoy it when I was a student".	I got a C in Shakespeare in college during a course in the English department. This horrified me because I was studying acting, and how could I get a C especially when I was doing much better in the theater department? The English professor asked us to analyze the text based on a concept that I must have missed in high school: imagery. I simply didn't understand what she meant by that. So my final paper for the English department was a disaster. Alas!

(Continued)

Table 3.1 (Continued)

Myth	Floyd's Facts
	But in the theater department, I felt the text. I relished the words in my mouth. The characters came to life in my voice and body. And I got an A.
	In the English department, I didn't understand the assignment and had to analyze it as only a great literary work but I didn't *feel* it. It felt outside me. The same is true today for students. If we only analyze it as a literary work instead of how it was intended, as a play, with action and emotion, students who study Shakespeare will feel that way, too, and dismiss a love of his work because an "AHA" moment never came for them.
	Shakespeare's plays are more akin to a musical score than a literary work. Approaching them that way will encourage an adventure that students will remember for the rest of their lives.
"Kids need to understand the history first".	Not really. Everything you need to know to act out the play is in the text with helpful hints provided in the acting scripts. Of course, you might decide to explore some of the historical elements, which can be very interesting.
	While historical knowledge isn't required to act out most of the plays, it would come in handy for *Henry V*, which is a history play. The battle of Agincourt, for example, is dramatized, and acting out the play will help students make meaning of the historical events. Our version of the play has all the information needed to do the play, including essential historical information.
"Shakespeare is boring".	Often true. If you just read the play! But if you speak it aloud and start moving around, playing the characters in an exciting plot; it becomes a whole new adventure. Where else can students plot to kill King Claudius in *Hamlet*? Rant and rave as a "green-eyed" monster in *Othello*? Stab Julius Caesar 23 times? Play the ghost of Hamlet's dead father? Or lead soldiers in a siege against the enemy in *Henry V*? These plot points are enjoyed by many middle school students. I think this is why I saw such high engagement for students who were known to struggle in the classroom when I was a teaching artist.

Shakespeare the Theater Guy

Today, William Shakespeare (1564–1616) is widely regarded as the greatest writer in the English language and the world's preeminent dramatist. His works have been translated into every major language, and his plays are produced more often than those of any other playwright. His works include:

- 37 plays
- 154 sonnets
- Several poems

Shakespeare's contemporaries would have laughed at the possibility that he would be regarded today as a genius. In his time, theaters were considered brothels and there was no standardized spelling until William Bullokar published *Brief Grammar for the English Language* in 1586.

Shakespeare was a theater guy: an actor, writer, and businessman who held shares in the Globe Theatre and acted in some of the productions of his plays. It is not known exactly how many roles Shakespeare played himself, though it is widely assumed that he played smaller roles in several of his own plays, including:

- *As You Like It* (Adam)
- *Macbeth* (King Duncan)
- *Henry IV* (King Henry)
- *Hamlet* (the Ghost of Hamlet's father)

While Shakespeare is often referred to as "The Bard of Avon" (or more simply, "The Bard") – so named as England's national poet – he entered life's stage as a man of the theater until his death on April 23, 1616.

The Globe and Other Theaters of Shakespeare's England

The first permanent theater of Shakespeare's England, called The Theater, was built in 1576, when Shakespeare was 12 years old. Shakespeare and his acting troupe, known as the Lord Chamberlain's Men, performed mostly at The Theater from 1594–1599 when they had become the most popular in England (they were later renamed the King's Men when King James adopted them after 1603). Because there are no surviving sketches, no one really knows what The Theater looked like.

The Theater was dismantled and moved across the Thames River to Southwark because of a dispute with the landlord. Six months later, it was rebuilt and renamed The Globe. By 1600, there were so many theaters in England that it became the most theatrical capitol in Europe! Some of the others included:

◆ The Curtain
◆ The Swan
◆ The Rose
◆ The Red Bull

The Globe burned down in 1613 during a performance of *Henry VIII* because a theatrical cannon misfired. It was rebuilt in 1614 but was closed by the Puritans along with all the other theaters in 1642 because, as they put it, plays stimulated "whorish lust".

Shakespeare's Language

What's Old English and What's Not

Because Shakespeare lived and wrote over four hundred years ago, his writing is often confused with Old English, which was spoken by the Anglo-Saxons who lived in what is now known as southern Denmark and northern Germany. Shakespeare did not write Old English, but Early Modern English. Here's a brief look at the evolution of the English language:

Old English: A.D. 449-1066
(think *Beowulf*, author unknown)
▼
Middle English: 1066-1450
(think *The Canterbury Tales* by Chaucer)
▼
Early Modern English: 1450-1660
▼
Later Modern English: 1660-today

Shakespeare's plays are considered Modern English because he lived from 1564–1616.

When instructing students, it can be enough to refer to Shakespeare as *modern English* and today as *contemporary English*. Alternatively, referring to Shakespeare's plays as *Sixteen Century English* always works.

Thee, You, and Wherefore

It might come as a surprise, but *you* was the formal personal pronoun in Renaissance England. *Thee* was the informal *you*. *Thy* was the informal *yours*.

That means that a fellow friend in Shakespeare's England would address his peers with *thee* and *thy* and address a person higher in status as *you*.

While we're at it, *wherefore* means *why*. It does not mean *where*. In the below example, Juliet asks:

> O Romeo, Romeo! Wherefore art thou Romeo?

Juliet is inquiring into why Romeo is a *Montague* – an enemy of her family. See the glossary for more definitions and word usage.

Shakespeare's Vocabulary

According to Doug Moston in *The First Folio of Shakespeare 1623*, "The King James Bible makes use of nearly 8,000 words. An educated person in our lifetime uses about 17,000 words. Contrast these figures with the number in Shakespeare's vocabulary – some 34,000. He used words in ingenious ways, employing nouns as verbs and inventing new words …. He actually invented over 1,700 words which appear for the first time in his writing". Others estimate Shakespeare introduced from 1,500 to 3,000 words into the English language.

Shakespeare coined the following words, which appear in the full-length version of the play indicated below but did not appear in the abridged acting scripts available for download (sorry about that!) with the exception of *tranquil* from *Othello*:

addiction: *Henry V* (Act 1, Scene 1)
buzzers: *Hamlet* (Act 4, Scene 5)
dawn: *Henry V* (Act 4, Scene 1)
inaudible[1]: *All's Well that Ends Well* (Act V, Scene 3)
elbow: *Henry V* (Act 3, Scene 4)
excitements: *Hamlet* (Act 4, Scene 4)
hint: *Othello* (Act 1, Scene 3)
majestic: *Julius Caesar* (Act 1, Scene 2)
outbreak: *Hamlet* (Act 2, Scene 1)
pander: *Hamlet* (Act 3, Scene 4)
rant: *Hamlet* (Act 5, Scene 1)
tranquil: *Othello* (Act 3, Scene 3)

Since many of the above words do not appear in the student scripts but might make compelling additions to a word wall, perhaps the students could do a word search activity in which they locate the word in the full-length version of the play. Alternatively, you or your students might find places to reinsert the lines in which the words appear.

Relishing Repetitions

The way Shakespeare puts sounds together is how he conveys meaning similarly to music. Using *Romeo and Juliet* as an example, "Romeo" ends in a legato vowel. "Juliet" ends in a staccato consonant. Just speaking the title of the play invokes conflict!

Shakespeare also tries to tell us something when he repeats sounds. Repeated consonants (alliteration) convey a character's thoughts and intellect; repeated vowels (assonance) convey feelings. Act 2, Scene 1 from *The Taming of the Shrew* has an excellent example of repeated consonants as in Kate's (the "shrew's") line when is speaking to Petruchio (the "tamer"):

> Well <u>h</u>ave you <u>h</u>eard, but something <u>h</u>ard of <u>h</u>earing.

John Basil in *Will Power: How to Act Shakespeare in 21 Days* observes, "In essence, she's laughing at Petruchio – 'Ha ha ha ha' – before correcting him". Basil is referencing the repetition of the *h* sound as an important clue to how to speak the line. In this way, the text resembles a musical score.

In Act 2, Scene 2 from *Henry V*, the conspiring Lord Scroop addresses his king who he is conspiring with others to murder:

> <u>S</u>o <u>s</u>ervice shall with <u>s</u>teeled <u>s</u>inews toil,
> And labour shall refresh itself with hope,
> To do your gra<u>c</u>e ince<u>ss</u>ant <u>s</u>ervice<u>s</u>.

While the sounds are not always in initial positions, it is difficult to dismiss the repetition of the *s* sound. If you speak the passage aloud, relishing the *s* each time it repeats, what does it remind you of? It's no mistake that Lord Scroop is hissing at Henry, unable to sustain the aural subterfuge of the plot to overthrow him.

Relishing repeating sounds will help students experience meaning through sound. Speaking inarticulately or rushing over the repetitions is like a movie without a soundtrack or with a very bad one. Full voicing of the vowels and consonants is important to work with Shakespeare's texts. When in doubt, take Hamlet's advice:

> Speak the speech, I pray you, as I pronounced it to
> you, trippingly on the tongue: but if you mouth it,
> as many of your players do, I had as lief[2] the
> town-crier spoke my lines.

If you hear every vowel and consonant from your students, then consider yourself on the right track. If not, encourage students to practice their lines until you can, coaching them to relish repeated vowels and consonants.

Learning Lines and Cue Scripts

Actors in Shakespeare's day had to learn their whole part in about a week. They didn't have several weeks of rehearsal like contemporary actors. A leading man could be required to learn up to 800 lines each day.

All the actor's lines were hand-written upon a roll of paper with a cue line, which is how actors' parts came to be known as a "role". The cue line was three or four words spoken by the character that came before, so the actors had to listen carefully to speak their lines in time.

Scrolls/rolls were returned to a bookkeeper before the play was performed and, on the occasion an actor couldn't learn all his lines, he might carry the roll onstage during the performance or rely on a backstage person to whisper lines into the actor's ear just before he was to enter.

On stage and off during a Shakespeare production, it was often hurly-burly, and the actors had to be good because the audience was often rowdy and would even throw food and drink at them if they didn't like the performance.

Gender

Women were not allowed to act until the year 1660, when Charles II demanded that females play women's parts. Before 1660, maidens fair and otherwise were played by boys who apprenticed in acting with adult males well-versed in acting:

> And if the boy have not a woman's gift
> To rain a shower of commanded tears,
> An onion will do well for such a shift,
> Which in a napkin being close conveyed
> Shall in despite enforce a watery eye.
> *- The Taming of the Shrew*

When acting Shakespeare with your students, girls and boys could play any part, regardless of gender. That means boys can play female parts; girls can play male parts; and gender nonbinary students can likewise play a gender with which they identify. It's up to you, and them, to make appropriate choices that deepen their connection to the story!

Please see Teaching Tip! for some fun facts about how theater was performed in Shakespeare's day.

> **Teaching Tip!**
>
> Two indispensable titles to learn more about Shakespeare's life, times, and plays are:
>
> ★ *The Complete Idiot's Guide to Shakespeare by* Laurie Rozakis
> ★ *Shakespeare for Dummies by* John Doyle and Ray Lischner
>
> Both were used as source material for this chapter and are excellent companions while staging it.

On Stage and Off: Fun Facts about Actor and Audience

- ◆ The theater operated under a repertory system, which means that actors would perform a different play each afternoon. That's right! *Hamlet* one day and *Julius Caesar* on another.
- ◆ Performances were from 2 pm to 5 pm, Monday through Saturday. Since electricity had not yet been invented, the actors had to perform when it was still light enough to see.
- ◆ There were no intermissions or restrooms. Imagine the atmosphere in the audience when nature calls after the first hour or so!
- ◆ The average run of a play was about ten performances. Popular plays would present more frequently.
- ◆ Although the stage had no curtains or sets, costumes were elaborate and often made from jewels, silk, and gold. Sometimes costumes were cast-offs from nobility.
- ◆ The actors had control of the production because there were no producers or directors.
- ◆ Prosperous women would sometimes attend performances but would wear a mask to hide their identities. Plays were, after all, entertainment for the lower classes, and no dignified lady would be seen at one.

Table 3.2 Acting Troupe Roles and Responsibilities

Players: were generally leading actors who owned a share of the company and were paid from the profits.

Hired Men: were actors who played smaller parts and hired by the day or the week for about a penny a day.

Bookkeeper: was hired to copy the play by hand. He managed all the scrolls containing the cue scripts and would prompt for lines when necessary.

Stage Keepers: managed props and kept the stage clean.

Tiremen: were responsible for the costumes.

Gatherers: collected the entrance money from the audience in boxes. Some research suggests that these boxes were placed in a room backstage as an early "box office", though the term doesn't appear in newspapers until the 18th century.

Apprentices: learned the technique of acting from a more experienced leading player.

Musicians: were hired to play sackbuts, an ancestor of the modern trombone.

Notes

1 Although *inaudible* appears in *All's Well that Ends Well*, which is not currently one of the plays in this series, the word is theatrically appropriate and too luscious to preclude.

2 Lief = willingly.

4

Scope and Sequence

While there are many ways in which you might approach staging a play in the school environment, this book recommends the following options:

1   One teacher stages all five Acts (more challenging), or
2   Five teachers across a whole grade each staging one Act (less challenging).

Alternatively, you might decide to do one Act without exploring any of the others. This can work, too! It's entirely up to you about how much material you would like to explore. Think of it like practicing a musical instrument: students practice and present as much material as time allows. It's up to you. The important thing is that students enter the field of play to make artistic choices about the characters they are playing.

Option #1 above will require more time and is reflected in Figure 4.1. Option #2 above will require less time but more collaboration with colleagues and is reflected in Figure 4.2.

The following scope and sequences are only recommendations. You might find that your students require lessons to happen at different times and at a different pace when you rehearse your play. That's okay! Doing a play is not an exact science and will require your creativity and judgment concerning what happens when.

DOI: 10.4324/9781003489733-4

Scope and Sequence

Before beginning the acting lessons, post your favorite Notable Quotations* from your chosen play in your classroom!

'Tis neither here nor there'.
–Emilia (Othello)

'Once more unto the breach!'
–King Henry (Henry V)

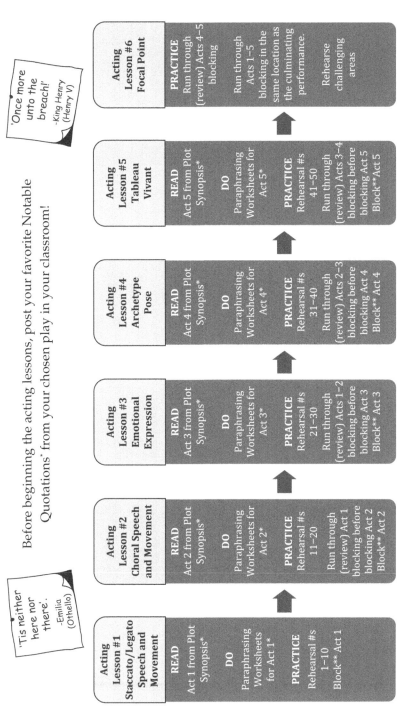

Acting Lesson #1 Staccato/Legato Speech and Movement

READ Act 1 from Plot Synopsis*

DO Paraphrasing Worksheets for Act 1*

PRACTICE Rehearsal #s 1–10
Block** Act 1

Acting Lesson #2 Choral Speech and Movement

READ Act 2 from Plot Synopsis*

DO Paraphrasing Worksheets for Act 2*

PRACTICE Rehearsal #s 11–20
Run through (review) Act 1 blocking before blocking Act 2
Block** Act 2

Acting Lesson #3 Emotional Expression

READ Act 3 from Plot Synopsis*

DO Paraphrasing Worksheets for Act 3*

PRACTICE Rehearsal #s 21–30
Run through (review) Acts 1–2 blocking before blocking Act 3
Block** Act 3

Acting Lesson #4 Archetype Pose

READ Act 4 from Plot Synopsis*

DO Paraphrasing Worksheets for Act 4*

PRACTICE Rehearsal #s 31–40
Run through (review) Acts 2–3 blocking before blocking Act 4
Block** Act 4

Acting Lesson #5 Tableau Vivant

READ Act 5 from Plot Synopsis*

DO Paraphrasing Worksheets for Act 5*

PRACTICE Rehearsal #s 41–50
Run through (review) Acts 3–4 blocking before blocking Act 5
Block** Act 5

Acting Lesson #6 Focal Point

PRACTICE Run through (review) Acts 4–5 blocking
Run through Acts 1–5 blocking in the same location as the culminating performance.
Rehearse challenging areas

Figure 4.1 Scope and Sequence Option #1: One Teacher Doing All Five Acts

FREE
INSTRUCTOR & STUDENT RESOURCES

* Paraphrasing worksheets are available for download and can be used as homework.
** block (noun): Pathways and positions on the stage that ensure actors can be seen.

Before beginning the acting lessons, post your favorite Notable
Quotations* from your chosen play in your classroom!

'Neither a
borrow nor a
lender be'.
-Polonius
(Hamlet)

'It was
Greek to me'.
-Casca
(Julius Caesar)

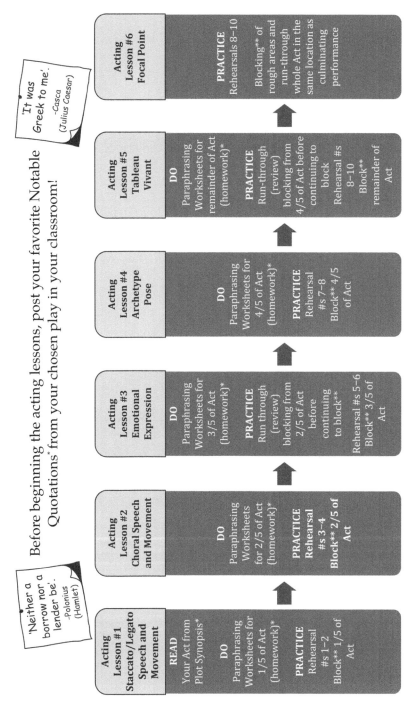

Acting Lesson #1 Staccato/Legato Speech and Movement

READ Your Act from Plot Synopsis*

DO Paraphrasing Worksheets for 1/5 of Act (homework)*

PRACTICE Rehearsal #s 1–2 Block** 1/5 of Act

Acting Lesson #2 Choral Speech and Movement

DO Paraphrasing Worksheets for 2/5 of Act (homework)*

PRACTICE Rehearsal #s 3–4 **Block** 2/5 of Act**

Acting Lesson #3 Emotional Expression

DO Paraphrasing Worksheets for 3/5 of Act (homework)*

PRACTICE Run through (review) blocking from 2/5 of Act before continuing to block** Rehearsal #s 5–6 Block** 3/5 of Act

Acting Lesson #4 Archetype Pose

DO Paraphrasing Worksheets for 4/5 of Act (homework)*

PRACTICE Rehearsal #s 7–8 Block** 4/5 of Act

Acting Lesson #5 Tableau Vivant

DO Paraphrasing Worksheets for remainder of Act (homework)*

PRACTICE Run-through (review) blocking from 4/5 of Act before continuing to block Rehearsal #s 8–10 Block** remainder of Act

Acting Lesson #6 Focal Point

PRACTICE Rehearsals 8–10

Blocking** of rough areas and run-through whole Act in the same location as culminating performance

Figure 4.2 Scope and Sequence Option #2: One Teacher Doing One Act

FREE

INSTRUCTOR & STUDENT RESOURCES

* Available separately for download.

** block (noun): Pathways and positions on the stage that ensure actors can be seen

5

Acting Lesson Plans

Introduction

Lessons in this chapter could occur concurrently with the rehearsal process explored in Chapter 6 depending on time and interest. Please see Chapter 4 for more information about the following two options:

- ◆ One teacher doing all five Acts, or
- ◆ Up to five teachers across a whole grade doing one Act.

Stage It recommends that you conduct the following acting lessons while rehearsing your chosen play.

DOI: 10.4324/9781003489733-5

To deepen understanding about communicating character through speech, movement, stillness, and silence, classmates respond to peer presentations through an assessment process that publicly shares criteria. Because this chapter aims to get the students thinking deeply about the characters they play and responding critically to peer presentations, assessment and sample reflection questions are embedded.

Using the Acting Lesson Plans

The lesson plans are organized into:

◆ **Introduction:** This section is intended for you to deepen your knowledge and understanding of the concept and to frame the lesson for students. You will see a table like the one below recommending when to do the lesson:

	One teacher doing all five Acts	Up to five teachers each doing one Act
When to do this lesson:	Rehearsals 1–10	Rehearsals 1–2

The above table is only a recommendation! You might find that doing lessons at different times at a different pace better suits your needs.

◆ **Aims:** Essential student outcomes in knowing, understanding, and doing.
◆ **Materials/Teacher Preparation:** This aspect of each lesson plan should be reviewed in advance of the lesson so you can adequately prepare.
◆ **Vocabulary:** Developmentally appropriate definitions and word usage to which students should be introduced at the beginning of the lesson.

The above preparation components are followed by a five-step sequence in most lesson plans[1]:

◆ **Step ONE: Jumping Off – Introduction and Vocabulary**
   – Introduces class to the concept and new vocabulary
◆ **Step TWO: Acting Concept**
   – Engages the class in the activity

- ◆ **Step THREE: Sharing**
  - – Shares student work with peers
- ◆ **Step FOUR: Assessment**
  - – Engages students in a peer-to-peer feedback process
- ◆ **Step FIVE: Reflection and Discussion**
  - – Builds understanding of the concept through asking high- and low-inquiry questions with appropriate wait-time

The entire five-step process described above will require forty-five to sixty minutes, depending on the pace of the lesson and classroom size.

An attempt has been made with the lesson plans to be as explicit as possible. As a result, they are longer than working lesson plans. Your lesson planning process might require less information than what is provided here, depending on your needs.

Staccato/Legato Movement and Speech

	One teacher doing all five Acts	Up to five teachers each doing one Act
When to do this lesson:	Rehearsals 1–10	Rehearsals 1–2

Introduction

Shakespeare's plays are meant to be spoken aloud. In his day, audiences went to *hear* a play as much as they went to see one. Because plays can be like music if words are put together in a certain way, the sounds can transport you to a place and elicit feelings in the audience.

Today's visual culture also relies on sound and music, but visual effects in movies and multi-layered soundtracks can do what the human voice has done ever since the ancient Greek theater: paint vivid portraits and bring about strong feelings from the audience. In a way, the sophisticated technical effects of today are like the effects vowels and consonants would have had on audiences in Shakespeare's time. Just like music, language can elicit strong feelings if the words are put together with their aural effects in mind.

"Staccato" and "legato" are concepts borrowed from music. They are expressive extremes that enable students to make choices about how their characters speak and move.

In music, *staccato* refers to notes that are short and choppy. *Legato*, Italian for "tied together", means to sustain vowels in classical singing. Transferring these concepts to acting for students, Stage It recommends the following single-use, developmentally appropriate definitions:

- **Staccato:** adverb and adjective. Fast and sharp movement and speech. Staccato is not the total opposite of legato because staccato is always rapid.
- **Legato:** adverb and adjective. Smooth and flowing, quick or slow (in tempo) movement and speech. Legato is not the total opposite of staccato because legato can be rapid or slow.

See Table 5.1. Some of the example songs have both staccato and legato qualities, which can help students understand how combining the two can make it interesting for the audience.

Table 5.1 Examples of Staccato and Legato Songs

Staccato	Legato
"All About That Bass" by Meghan Trainor	"All of Me" by John Legend
"Baai" by Emmanuel Lai with Abdel Gadem Salem	"Boo'd Up" by Ella Mai
"Can't Hold Us" ft. Ray Dalton by Macklemore & Ryan Lewis	"Don't Know Why" by Norah Jones
"The Contemporary Fix" by Lindstrom	"Ocean Eyes" by Billie Eilish
"Harder, Better, Faster, Stronger" by Daft Punk	"Smooth Operator" by Sade
"Serra Pelada" by Philip Glass [a]	"Someone Like You" by Adele
"Single Ladies (Put a Ring on It)" by Beyoncé	"Vincent (Starry, Starry Night)" by Don McLean
"Uptown Funk" ft. Bruno Mars by Mark Ronson	"Yesterday" by The Beatles

[a] This song has the added benefit of children singing.

An excellent example of how combining the legato and staccato sounds can contribute to aural interest is in the song, "Legato Staccato" by Teresa Jennings (ASCAP):

https://www.musick8.com/store/alphadetail.php?product_group=1794 [2]

The short song begins with children singing legato, then staccato, and finally both legato and staccato. The simultaneous singing of legato and staccato at the end of the song creates an interesting contrast for the listener. This could be described as aural conflict.

Shakespeare was acutely aware of the aural effects of putting sounds together. One of the best legato and staccato examples is from one of his most famous plays. While *Romeo and Juliet* is not included in the Stage It series of plays available for download, it is an excellent example of how the musicality of words conveys meaning.

Practice speaking the following words aloud:

- Romeo
- Benvolio
- Mercutio

Now say each of the following aloud:

- Juliet
- Capulet
- Tybalt

What do you notice? Romeo and his family's names end in fluid ("legato") vowels. Juliet's family ends in sharp ("staccato") consonants. This was no accident! Shakespeare intended for the audience to *hear* conflict just by pronouncing the words. Just like with the "Legato Staccato" song by Teresa Jennings, the audience will feel the tension of the conflicting sounds even if the actors, or singers, do nothing more than speak the speech trippingly on their tongues.

Staccato/Legato Movement and Speech Lesson Plan

This activity helps students understand that staccato movement and speech are sharp and quick; legato movement and speech are smooth and connected. While rehearsing, these concepts can help them make choices about how their characters move and speak.

Students will:

- Understand that how an actor speaks and moves conveys meaning to an audience.
- Know that staccato and legato are among the choices an actor can make about movement and speech.
- Know that staccato is sharp and quick.
- Know that legato is smooth and connected.
- Know that tempo is the speed of something (like movement and speech).

◆ Be able to speak and move in a staccato and legato way.
◆ Respond critically to their classmates' ability to speak and move in a staccato and legato way.
◆ Reflect on their experience to extend their thinking.

For inquiry-based learning: Turn your instructional aims into a question and write the question on the board before engaging students in the activity. Throughout the lesson, encourage students to investigate possible responses to the question:

What information does speaking and moving in a staccato or legato way convey to an audience?

Materials/Teacher Preparation

◆ An audio player or mobile device that can play music cued up to share the "Legato Staccato" song by Teresa Jennings.
◆ Self-Assessment chart "Legato/Staccato" written on poster board or the blackboard.
◆ Marker for tallying numbers.

Vocabulary

◆ **Legato** (adverb and adjective): Smooth, quick, or slow (in tempo) movement and speech.
◆ **Staccato** (adverb and adjective): Sharp, quick movement, and speech.
◆ **Tempo** (noun): Speed of something.

> **Teaching Tip!**
>
> Legato and staccato are only partial opposites. While staccato is sharp and legato is smooth, each has a different *tempo*. Staccato is quick, and legato can be fast or slow.

Please see Figure 5.1 for examples of legato and staccato songs.

Step ONE: Jumping Off – Introduction and Vocabulary

1 While in front of the class, advise the students that they are about to learn a basic acting skill about movement and speaking.

2 Advise the students that "legato" means smooth and connected and "staccato" means sharp and quick movement and speech. Music students might recognize these words because we are borrowing them from music!

3 Advise students that *tempo* refers to the speed at which something is moving. Staccato movement and speech, for example, is always fast. Legato movement and speech can be fast or slow.

4 While standing at the front of the room, demonstrate sharp and quick movement and speech by speaking aloud "staccato" rapidly and sharply while also gesturing in a quick and fast way. Pause. Then demonstrate smooth and connected movement and speech by speaking aloud "legato" while also gesturing in a smooth and connected way.

5 Tell students that they are now going to participate in an activity so they can experience these ideas.

Step TWO: Experiencing Staccato Speaking and Moving

1 Split the classroom into two large groups. Then assign one side of the room "legato: smooth and connected" and the other side of the room "staccato: sharp and quick".

2 Ask the staccato side of the room to stand with the other side of the room to remain in their chairs as audience members.

3 Ask the staccato side of the room to speak the word, "Staccato", while also moving their bodies in a sharp and rapid way when you give the cue, "3-2-1-ACTION!".

4 Give the cue, "3-2-1-ACTION", while the students give it a go.

5 (If needed) Coach students, *Let's try it again but see if you can make your speech and gestures even sharper! Try to speak and move together as much as possible so we can understand what you are saying.*

6 Tell students, *I am now going to ask the other side of the room to give the action cue, "3-2-1-Action!"*

7 Ask the other side of the room to give the action cue, "3-2-1-Action!" so the staccato side of the room can do it again.

Teaching Tip!

When teaching in an English Language Learner classroom, I was asked by students why I wanted them to move like a cat. I had no idea why they asked that question until one of them told me that the Spanish translation of "the cat" is "el gato", which sounds a lot like "legato".

Italian for "the cat" is "il gatto" and Portuguese is "o gato".

Perhaps I should have articulated my words better! When teaching English Language Learners, remember to speak clearly and remain mindful that students might hear one word when you mean another.

Step THREE: Staccato Assessment

1   After the staccato side of the room has spoken, "staccato", while moving in a sharp and rapid way, ask the other side of the room to look at the assessment you've written on the board and critique the staccato presentation with a show of hands whether the presenting students moved and spoke sharply (Table 5.2):

Table 5.2 STACCATO: Sharp and Quick Assessment

	STACCATO: Sharp and Quick			
	Poor (1) None	Fair (2) Some	Good (3) Most	Masterful (4) All
Movement				
Speech				

2   Begin with "Masterful" and ask the audience of classmates if they saw and heard the staccato actors move and speak in a sharp way. Quickly count the number of responders and record that number in the appropriate box. Ask the audience of classmates why they responded the way they did for each team and what the staccato actors could do better next time. Remind the students that this is not a competition but a process to help them learn how to critique each other's work while working together.

3   Ask the audience of classmates *What did you see? Were the gestures sharp and quick? Was the speech sharp and quick? What did this kind of movement and speech convey to you as an audience? What kind of character or person moves and speaks in this way*? Encourage discussion and diverse interpretations – all of which are correct if students can logically support their interpretation with what they saw and heard.

4   Tell the students that they will now reverse roles as the staccato side of the room becomes the audience and the legato side of the room becomes the actors.

Step FOUR: Experiencing Legato Speaking and Moving

1   Ask the staccato side of the room to sit if they aren't already, and ask the legato side of the room to stand beside their desks. Ask the staccato side of the room to stand with the other side of the room to remain in their chairs as audience members.

2   Ask the legato side of the room to speak the word, "Legato", while also moving their bodies in a smooth and connected way when you give the cue, "3-2-1-ACTION!".

3   Give the cue, "3-2-1-ACTION", while the students give it a go.
4   (If needed) Coach students, *Let's try it again but see if you can make your speech and gestures even smoother! Try to speak and move together as much as possible so we can understand what you are saying.*
5   Tell students, *I am now going to ask the other side of the room to give the action cue, "3-2-1-Action!"*
6   Ask the staccato side of the room to give the action cue, "3-2-1-Action!" so the legato side of the room can do it again.

Step FIVE: Legato Assessment

1   After the legato side of the room has spoken, "legato", while moving in a smooth and connected way, ask the staccato side of the room to look at the assessment you've written on the board and critique the legato presentation with a show of hands whether the presenting students moved and spoke in a smooth and connected way (Table 5.3).

Table 5.3 LEGATO: Smooth and Connected Assessment

	LEGATO: Smooth and Connected			
	Poor (1) **None**	**Fair (2)** **Some**	**Good (3)** **Most**	**Masterful (4)** **All**
Movement				
Speech				

2   Begin with "Masterful" and ask the audience of classmates if they saw and heard the legato actors move and speak in a smooth and connected way. Quickly count the number of responders and record that number in the appropriate box. Ask the audience of classmates why they responded the way they did for each team and what the legato actors could do better next time. Remind the students that this is not a competition but a process to help them learn how to critique each other's work while working together.
3   Ask the audience of classmates *What did you see? Were the gestures smooth and connected? Was the speech smooth and connected? What did this kind of movement and speech convey to you as an audience? What kind of character or person moves and speaks in this way?* Encourage discussion and diverse interpretations – all of which are correct if students can logically support their interpretation with what they saw and heard.
4   Tell the students that they will now reflect.

Step SIX: Reflection

Lead a reflective discussion with the following questions (give students time to think about their responses)[3]:

◆ Did the staccato/legato presentations today convey sharp and quickly and smooth and connected? Why or why not? How do you know?
  – *Any answer is correct if it relates to what the student did, saw, and/or thought.*

◆ Have you seen or heard someone in your life or in the news move or speak in a staccato way? Legato way? Why do you think they are moving or speaking in this way? What does it tell you about them?
  – *Any answer is correct if it relates to what the student did, saw, and/or thought.*

◆ Do you think some people might sometimes move and speak in a legato way and, at other times, in a legato way? Why do you think this happens?
  – *Events going on around a person can often affect how they speak and move. For example, a person late to a birthday party might move and speak in a staccato way because they are in a hurry. That same person might move and speak in a legato way after they arrive at the party because they are no longer in a hurry.*

◆ Why do you think it is important for an actor to be able to move and speak in different ways?
  – *People and characters move and speak in different ways. A soldier, for example, might move and speak in a staccato way during basic training. A father might sing to his baby in a legato way to help the child sleep. A good actor must be able to express these different ways of being.*

◆ Where else do you see staccato movement and speech? What about legato?
  – *Staccato and legato examples are all around us! Just like the soldier or the father mentioned above, you might see and hear staccato in the rapid downfall of rain accompanied by the sound of smooth and connected wind.*

◆ What examples of staccato and legato do you recognize in the school, your neighborhood, or on TV?

  Staccato:

  – *People in a hurry.*
  – *Alex Dunphy (Modern Family): Alex is known for her quick thinking and sharp intellect. Her dialogue and movements often reflect a more staccato quality.*

  – *SpongeBob SquarePants (SpongeBob SquarePants): SpongeBob often exhibits quick, energetic, and staccato movements, especially when he's excited or in a hurry.*
  – *Tigger (Winnie the Pooh): Tigger's bouncing and energetic personality can be seen as staccato, with quick and lively movements.*
  – *Road Runner (Looney Tunes): The Road Runner is known for its rapid movements and quick escapes!*

  Legato:

  – *People relaxed and easygoing.*
  – *Elena Gilbert (The Vampire Diaries): Elena's character tends to have a more serene and thoughtful quality, with smoother movements and a legato style of speech.*
  – *Mickey Mouse (Mickey Mouse Clubhouse): Mickey's movements and speech are generally smooth and flowing.*
  – *Pooh Bear (Winnie the Pooh): Winnie the Pooh's calm and laid-back nature often results in legato movements and a slow, deliberate way of speaking.*
  – *Kuzco (The Emperor's New School): Kuzco's character often moves in a relaxed, smooth manner, especially when he's in his "cool" mode.*

◆ What are the benefits of studying how an actor moves and speaks in different ways?
  – *Knowing and being able to move in different ways enables an actor to play different kinds of characters.*
◆ What did you find most surprising about moving and speaking in a staccato or legato way?
  – *Any answer is correct if it relates to what the student did and/or thought.*

Wrap up by sharing, *Next time, we're going to deepen our understanding of moving and speaking together based on a theatrical tradition that goes back thousands of years. Yes! That's right – we did a little bit of that today but next time we'll explore choral speaking and moving based on the ancient Greeks.*

Choral Speaking and Moving

	One teacher doing all five Acts	Up to five teachers each doing one Act
When to do this lesson:	Rehearsals 11–20[4]	Rehearsals 3–4

Introduction

The tradition of moving and speaking in unison is attributed to the ancient Greek chorus. All surviving Greek plays had a chorus, which would often provide essential information for the audience to understand the play.

The purpose of the chorus in ancient Greece often involved commenting on the themes, actions, messages, and ideas of the play. Choruses can also express characters' inner thoughts while providing an aural experience for the audience that draws them in. The Stage It approach involves:

◆ **Chorus:** Each of the acting scripts in the Stage It series has a Chorus, which serves a similar function as the Greek chorus. The Chorus sometimes "comments" on the action but often amplifies messages and ideas in the play to help advance the plot. For example, the Stage It edition of *Hamlet* reassigns some of Hamlet's lines in the full-length version to a Chorus to amplify the ideas:

87. **Hamlet:** What a piece of work[5] is a man. How noble in reason.

88. **Chorus:** **How infinite in faculties[6]! In form and moving how express[7] and admirable.**

89. **Hamlet:** In action how like an angel.

90. **Chorus:** **In apprehension[8] how like a god.**

91. **Hamlet:** And yet, to me, what is this quintessence[9] of dust?[10] Man delights not me.

◆ **Choral Character Teams:** The Stage It approach to casting students in roles recommends that each character be played by several students. Students at this age generally love to work in teams, and choral character teams are a great way to appeal to this stage of children's development. In the above example, Hamlet's lines 87, 89, and 91 would be played by a group of students playing Hamlet.

The choral character approach also applies to all characters in the play. Using multiple students in the same role is recommended because it solves several challenges of a school play with a whole classroom of students (Table 5.4):

◆ Several students speaking together make it easier for the audience to hear.

◆ Several students moving together make them easier for the audience to see.

Table 5.4 Modern Examples of Choral Speaking and Moving

Adult Example	Children's Example
Mighty Aphrodite (1995) The Woody Allen film opens with a scene of the ancient theater in Taormina, Sicily with a Greek chorus introducing and narrating the story. While this film is not appropriate for students at this age, the film makes use of the Chorus in similar ways to Stage It and is a good example for adult teachers to think about the concept.	Disney's *Hercules* (1997) The "muses" in opening credits of Disney's 1997 animated version of *Hercules* are a good example of singing and moving in unison while commenting/introducing the story to help contextualize the Greek hero's journey.

- The culminating performance of the play will still go on even if a student is absent on the day of the show.
- It's fun to work together in teams, especially for this age group!

Choral Speaking and Moving Lesson Plan

This lesson will build students' understanding of the importance of working together in teams while increasing audibility.

Students will:

- Be able to speak and move together.
- Know that choral speaking and moving originated in ancient Greece.
- Know that choral speaking increases audibility.
- Understand that working together as a team makes the whole performance better.

Inquiry:

What are the benefits of choral speaking and moving?

Materials/Teacher Preparation

- 5–6 index cards each with a different line of text from your chosen Stage It play (or you could write each line on the blackboard or Smartboard).
- Self-Assessment chart "Choral Speaking and Moving" written on poster board or the blackboard.
- Marker or chalk for tallying numbers.

Vocabulary

- **Chorus** (noun): A group of actors speaking and moving in unison.
- **Choral Character Team** (noun phrase): Multiple students playing the same character often speaking and moving in unison.
- **Unison** (noun): Performance of action or speech together.
- **Audible** (adjective): Being heard.
- **Gesture** (noun): A single movement of part of the body.
- **Action** (noun): Something the character does usually described as a verb.
- **Articulate** (verb): To pronounce words clearly. Articulators include lips, teeth, and tongue.
- **Cue** (noun): A signal for an actor to begin something.
- **Neutral position** (adjective modifying a noun): Physical state of readiness to receive instruction or direction. The visible behavior of readiness: two feet flat on the floor, arms down at the side, silent, and focused.

> **Teaching Tip!**
>
> If students are struggling to articulate their words, ask them to pronounce the consonants with a more *staccato* quality.
>
> The sharp and quick speech will encourage them to energize their speaking.

Step ONE: Jumping Off – Introduction and Vocabulary

1. While in front of the class, advise the students that they are about to learn an acting skill that dates back thousands of years!
2. Advise the students that a Chorus of actors is like a chorus of singers: they speak, sing, and move together.
3. Advise students that speaking and moving together require practice, and even professional actors will have to repeat their phrases over and over to get everyone together.

Step TWO: Experiencing Choral Speaking and Moving

1. Break students into character teams of four or five in each group.
2. Distribute one card to each team with different lines of text from your chosen Stage It play on each card. Select different lines of text for each team. See Table 5.5. The most effective lines for this lesson will be brief and no longer than one or two sentences.
3. Have students brainstorm for five minutes about how they might move and speak their line together. Ask, *What clues might be in your line to help you figure out how to speak and move?*

Table 5.5 Example Line Assignments from *Julius Caesar* for Choral Speaking and Moving [a]

Choral Character Team #	Choral Character Team and Pronunciation	Line
1	Chorus (KAW-ruhs)	O Caesar. Great Caesar.
2	Caesar (SEE-zer)[b]	Doth[c] not Brutus[d] bootless[e] kneel?
3	Casca (KAAS-kuh)[f]	Speak, hands, for me!
4	Caesar	Et tu, Brute?[g] Then fall Caesar. *(Caesar dies)*
5	Chorus (KAW-ruhs)	Liberty! Freedom! Tyranny is dead!

[a] Lines from *Julius Caesar* are shared as an example. Please select whatever lines you like from the play of your choice. For this lesson, short lines are recommended for now because the focus is on speaking and moving together. Interpreting the lines will come later.

[b] Roman emperor.

[c] doth (DUHTH) (verb): Do or does.

[d] Brutus (BROO-tuhs): One of the Caesar's closest friends.

[e] bootless: uselessly.

[f] Casca is the first to stab Caesar.

[g] et tu, Brute: Latin for *even you, Brutus*.

4 Have students collaborate and agree on one gesture that everyone in the group will do together. Let them imagine and be creative! Advise the students, *Think about using whatever gesture you decide on as a way to begin and end together. Don't forget to speak as clearly as you can by beginning and ending your speech together as well!*

5 Tell students, *It might be helpful for a member of each team to cue the other members of the team to begin by whispering quietly, "3-2-1-Action". This is not required, though, because you might find a better way to cue your teammates.*

6 Remind students that a cue is a signal for an actor to begin something.

7 Clarify for students that:

a they should work together (listen to each other respectfully, respond to their peers) because you will look for evidence of collaboration when they share their work with the class;

Teaching Tip!

Do a read-aloud of the plot synopsis for your chosen play provided in the downloadable Stage It edition before engaging in this lesson. The plot synopsis will give your students a basic understanding of the characters and main actions of the plot. See Chapter 4.

b the criterion for assessment is everyone in the team speaking and moving together when they share their work with the class;

c the activity has a structure:
  1 beginning (a neutral position)
  2 middle (gesturing and speaking)
  3 end (holding in stillness at the end for three seconds)

Step THREE: Sharing Your Movement and Speech

1 Have students recall that working together is important in theater because actors must rely on each other.
2 Have each team share its line of text using the same presentation structure. Teams can present in any order you like.
3 Remind students that team members begin in a neutral position. See Figure 5.1.
4 Keep time as students hold in stillness at the end for at least three seconds. Students may come back to a neutral position at the end of their presentation.
5 Ask the audience of classmates, *What did you see? Did everyone speak together? Move together? How do you know?* Encourage discussion and diverse interpretations – all of which are correct if students can logically support their interpretation with what they saw and heard.

Step FOUR: Assessment of Presentation

1 Ask the audience of classmates to look at the assessment you've written on the board and critique team by team with a show of hands whether all students in each team were able to speak and move together (Table 5.6). See Table 5.7 for assessment options.
2 Begin with "Masterful" and ask the audience of classmates if they saw all the actors in the team speak together. Quickly count the number of responders and record that number in the appropriate box.

Table 5.6 Choral Speaking and Moving Assessment

	CHORAL SPEAKING AND MOVING			
	Poor (1) **None**	**Fair (2)** **Some**	**Good (3)** **Most**	**Masterful (4)** **All**
Speaking				
Moving				

3 Begin with "Masterful" and ask the audience of classmates if they saw all the actors in the team move together. Quickly count the number of responders and record that number in the appropriate box.

4 Ask the audience of classmates why they responded the way they did for each team and what the team can do better next time. Continue asking the same question for each team and filling in the score until all the teams have presented. Remind the students that this is not a competition but a process to help them learn how to critique each other's work while working together.

5 If students scored more ones and twos than they did threes and fours, it is a good idea to offer them another go at it. Remember that acting requires practice! **This process is not about perfection but about teaching the students how to practice something**. The students should stick to the indicator of all members of their team speaking and moving together as a measure of success – not what they "liked" or "did not like".

6 Encourage feedback to the whole team instead of individual actors within the team. Keep the pace of assessment rapid and flowing.

The following *Two Feet* poem is a call-and-response activity that you can use to get the students' attention and is particularly helpful at the beginning of each lesson or at any time in the process as a classroom management tool. If the children get too rambunctious, use this call-and-response to get them focused and ready for the next instruction. In Stages of Learning classrooms, this was sometimes referred to as "ready position".

After speaking one line, allow the children to repeat it in unison before moving on to the next line. It is okay for them to gesture while speaking the lines so long as they are focused and silent by the end. Albert R. I. Elias, Founder, Director of Creative Stages NYC, llc., who uses the Stage It techniques in his classrooms to this day, often translates the poem for his Spanish-speaking students:

English	Spanish[*]
Two feet flat on the floor	*Dos pies plantados en el suelo*
Arms down at my side	*Brasos en ambos lados*
My belly deep and wide	*Mi vientre ancho y profundo*
Two feet ready to explore	*Dos pies listos a explorar*
Two arms ready to fly	*Dos brazos listos a volar*
My belly deep as sea	*Mi vientre profundo como el mar*
My mind vast as sky	*Mi mente vasta como el cielo*

It's also a great way to practice choral speaking. Teachers have even used it to help students focus prior to lessons in other subjects! It works, too, when the students are rambunctious and you want to get their attention.

Step FIVE: Reflection and Discussion

Lead a reflective discussion with the following questions:

◆ What are the benefits of working together in a group?
  – *Working together can help us all get better and support each other. If someone forgets a line, for example, the other students in the choral character team might remember it. Students can also help each other by choosing a gesture and a tone of voice for speaking.*
◆ Did the presentations today begin and end together? Why or why not? How do you know?
  – *Any answer is correct if it relates to what the student did, saw, and/or thought.*

[*] Spanish translation by Paco Arroyo.

◆ What was one of the hardest things about speaking and moving together?
  – *Beginning is often one of the hardest things to do, which is why professional actors need cues. Cues are signals to begin something. In movies, directors might say, "3-2-1-ACTION", which is an example of a cue, but the audience will not know about that. What are some other ways that each choral character team could cue themselves to begin?* [11]

◆ Why do you think it's important to learn to move and speak together in theater?
  – *Speaking and moving together means that the audience will be able to see the movements and hear the words more easily. It's also helpful in case a student actor is not able to attend the culminating performance of the play: we will still have several actors in each role to ensure the play goes on!*

◆ What did you learn from speaking and moving together?
  – *Any answer is correct if it relates to what the student did and/or thought.*

◆ What did you find most surprising about speaking and moving together?
  – *Any answer is correct if it relates to what the student did and/or thought.*

Wrap up by sharing, *Next time, we're going to explore how an actor expresses emotion through speaking and moving!*

Figure 5.1 Neutral position and neutral position mini-lesson. (Illustration by Ian Dale.)

Table 5.7 Additional Choral Speaking and Moving Indicators

Poor	Fair	Good	Excellent
1 Few to no consonants begin and end together. 2 Few to no words are audible. 3 None of the actors speak at the same tempo. 4 No gestures begin and end together. 5 None of the actors use the same gesture.	1 Some consonants begin and end together. 2 Some words are audible. 3 Some actors speak at the same tempo. 4 Some gestures begin and end together. 5 Some actors use the same gesture.	1 Most consonants begin and end together. 2 Most words are audible. 3 Most actors speak at the same tempo. 4 Most gestures begin and end together. 5 Most actors use the same gesture.	1 All consonants begin and end together. 2 All words are audible. 3 All actors speak at the same tempo. 4 All gestures begin and end together. 5 All actors use the same gesture.

Emotional Expression (8 Basic Emotions)

"Your face, my thane, is as a book where men may read strange matters".

- Lady Macbeth

	One teacher doing all five Acts	Up to five teachers each doing one Act
When to do this lesson:	Rehearsals 21–30[12]	Rehearsals 5–6

While we wise and well-lived adults may have integrated life experience into our thinking along with an understanding of their accompanying emotions, children are just learning that emotions exist and have names. Put another way, we adults might be able to "read" emotions of the face and the voice, but children are learning to do this just like reading words on a page and understanding their meaning.

The process of "reading" emotions of the face and voice could be called "emotional literacy" or "emotional intelligence", which is defined as:

The ability to perceive, use, understand, manage, and handle emotions. People with high emotional intelligence can recognize their own emotions and those of others, use emotional information to guide thinking and behavior, discern between different feelings and label them appropriately, and adjust emotions to adapt to environments.[13]

Professional actors are trained in "perceiving, using, understanding, and managing emotions" from the first day they step into an acting studio through the final bow after a performance. Acting is the domain of emotions and engenders a deep sense of belonging for children who developmentally are curious about how to appropriately express and "read" them.

Dr. Robert Plutchik, a professor and psychologist who published a "wheel of emotions" in 1980, indicated eight primary emotions[14]:

◆ Anger   ◆ Joy   ◆ Surprise
◆ Fear   ◆ Disgust   ◆ Trust
◆ Sadness   ◆ Anticipation

According to Dr. Plutchik, all other emotions occur as combinations of the primary emotions. "For example, anticipation and joy combine to be optimism. Joy and trust combine to be love. Emotions are often complex, and being able to recognize when a feeling is actually a combination of two or more distinct feelings is a helpful skill".[15]

Dr. Plutchik's basic eight is a great place to begin! As with reading words on a page, "reading" the emotions of others takes practice. Expressing them requires the same.

Emotional Expression Lesson Plan

This activity builds an understanding of eight basic emotions by exploring what they look and sound like. There could be lots of laughs and giggles during this lesson and that's okay. The key point here is for children to understand that emotions have names and that actors must be able to recognize them in others and express them at appropriate times through the voice and body.

Students will:

◆ Know how to express and recognize emotions on the face.
◆ Know how to express and recognize emotions through the voice.
◆ Collaboratively analyze a section of text for clues into what a character is feeling.
◆ Assess peer presentations and provide feedback based on shared criteria.
◆ Understand that there are many emotions comprised of combinations of the basic 8.
◆ Reflect and discuss what they learned as actors and as audiences.

For inquiry-based learning: turn your instructional aims into a question and write the question on the board before engaging students in the activity. Throughout the lesson, encourage students to investigate possible responses to the question:

How does an actor convey emotion to an audience?

Materials/Teacher Preparation

- ◆ Write the eight basic emotions on the blackboard or smart board.
- ◆ Five to six index cards each with a different line of text from your chosen Stage It play.
- ◆ A line of text from your chosen Stage It play written on the blackboard or smart board for you to demonstrate.
- ◆ Self-Assessment chart "Expressing Emotion" written on poster board, blackboard, or smartboard.
- ◆ Marker or chalk for tallying numbers.

Vocabulary

- ◆ **Emotion** (noun): A feeling.
- ◆ **Expression**. (noun): The process of making known your thoughts or feelings.
- ◆ **Tone** (noun): A vocal sound.

Step ONE: Jumping Off – Introduction and Vocabulary

1   Tell the students, *Today, we are going to explore how an actor expresses emotions. There are eight basic emotions: anger, fear, sadness, joy, disgust, anticipation, surprise, and trust. We won't experience all eight today, but we will probably experience them as we rehearse our play.*
2   In front of the class, stand silently and perfectly still in a neutral position. Tell the students, *I am going to demonstrate how an actor expresses emotion through the voice and face by reading a line of text from our play first without emotion and then with it. I am going to play the part of* [select one character from Table 5.8 for suggestions from each of the four plays].

Table 5.8 Emotional Expression Examples for Teacher Demonstration

Character	Play	Line #	Line	Recommended Emotion
Roderigo (RAH-duh-REE-goh): A pawn of the evil villain of the play.	*Othello*	11	I'll call aloud. Awake! What ho, Thieves! Thieves!	Fear
Ely (EE-lee) He is a bishop, who is a religious leader, and very powerful in the kingdom.	*Henry V*	18	I long to hear it!	Anticipation
Hamlet (HAAM-lit) Prince of Denmark and son of the recently murdered King Claudius.	*Hamlet*	79	You are a fishmonger. [a]	Disgust
Chorus (KAW-ruhs)	*Julius Caesar*	6	Beware the ides of March. [b]	Fear

[a] Fishmonger: someone who sells fish.

[b] Ides of March: March 15.

3 Then read your line of text without expression. Pause. Then read the line of text with emotion in your face and voice. At the end of your presentation, hold the expression for a second or two so students can take it in. Then return to the neutral position.

4 Ask students if they were able to detect an emotion in your voice or face. *What was I expressing? How do you know? What did my face look like? What tone did you hear in my voice? Now you are going to do the same thing in groups!*

Step TWO: Expressing Emotion through the Face and Voice

1 Break students into character teams of four or five in each group.

2 Distribute one emotional expression card to each team with a different line of text from your chosen play on each card. See Table 5.8.1 for an example from *Julius Caesar.*

Table 5.8.1 Example Using *Julius Caesar*

Character	Line #	Line to Write on Index Card	Possible Emotions to Coach
Chorus (KAW-ruhs)	6	Beware the ides of March. [a]	Anticipation/Fear
Caesar (SEE-zer)	8	He is a dreamer. Let us leave him.	Anticipation
Chorus (KAW-ruhs)	18	Cry havoc![b] and let slip the dogs of war.	Anger
Chorus (KAW-ruhs)	39	There's a bargain made.	Trust
Chorus (KAW-ruhs)	105	Here comes his body mourned by Mark Antony.[c]	Sadness

[a] Ides of March: March 15.

[b] Havoc (noun): devastation and chaos.

[c] Mark Antony (AAN-tuh-nee): One of Julius Caesar's closest friends.

3   Have students brainstorm for five minutes about what emotion might work for the line of text. Let their imaginations go! Ask, *Once your team has agreed on an emotion, then practice speaking and moving in your choral character team to express that emotion on your face and in your voice. Remember to begin and end together.*

4   Have students collaborate and agree on one emotion that everyone in the group will do using their line of text. Coach, *Think about the expression on your face and the tone of voice you will use.*

5   Remind the students that:
   a   they should work together (listen to each other respectfully, respond to their peers) because you will look for evidence of collaboration when they share their work with the class;
   b   the criterion for assessment is everyone in the team expressing the same emotion through their face and voice when they share their work with the class;
   c   the activity has a structure:
      1   beginning (a neutral position)
      2   middle (expressing the emotion)
      3   end (holding at the end for one second)

Step THREE: Expressing Emotion

1   Have students recall how you presented an emotion at the beginning of class starting in a neutral position, expressing the emotion, and

then holding it for a second at the end so the audience of students could take it in. Have each team share their presentation using the same structure.

2 Explain that team members begin in a neutral position and end in a neutral position.

3 Ask the presenting team to come to the front of the classroom to present their work.

4 Ask the audience of classmates, *What did you see? What did you hear?* Encourage discussion and diverse interpretations – all of which are correct if students can logically support their interpretation with what they saw.

Step FOUR: Assessment of Emotional Expression

1 Remind the students that it is important for actors in theater to work together toward a common goal because without it there is no sense of ensemble and a feeling of the whole.

2 Ask the audience of classmates to look at the assessment you've written on the board and critique team by team with a show of hands whether all actors in each team expressed emotion through their voices and faces (Table 5.8.2):

Table 5.8.2 Emotional Expression Assessment

	Emotional Expression			
	Poor (1) **None**	**Fair (2)** **Some**	**Good (3)** **Most**	**Masterful (4)** **All**
1. Face				
2. Voice				

3 Begin with "Masterful" and ask the audience of classmates if they saw and heard all students in the team remain in the same pose for five seconds. Quickly count the number of responders and record that number in the appropriate box. Ask the audience of classmates why they responded the way they did for each team and what the team can do better next time. Continue asking the same question for each team and filling in the score until all the teams have presented. Remind the students that this is not a competition but a process to help them learn how to critique each other's work while working together.

4 If students scored more ones and twos than they did threes and fours, it is a good idea to offer them another go at it. Remember that acting requires practice! The students should stick to the indicator of all members of their team sustaining stillness as a measure of success – not what they "liked" or "did not like".

5 Encourage feedback to the whole team instead of individual actors within the team. Keep the pace of assessment rapid and flowing.

Step FIVE: Reflection and Discussion

Lead a reflective discussion with the following questions:

◆ How does an actor convey emotion?
  – *The face and voice are essential conveyors of emotion. Students might come up with other ways to express emotions and any answer is correct if it relates to what the student did, saw, and/or thought. This is a good time to remind students that if the emotions of the character they are playing are important for the audience, then their faces will need to be visible and their voices audible.*

◆ Did the presentations today convey what the students were trying to communicate? Why or why not? How do you know?
  – *Any answer is correct if it relates to what the student did, saw, and/or thought.*

◆ Why do you think it is important for an actor to be able to express emotions?
  – *If an actor's interpretation stays in their head, then the audience can't see it or hear it and may not understand what the character is feeling. Acting is about making the actor's interpretation of a character visible and audible to an audience and emotional expression is one example.*

◆ What are the benefits of studying how an actor expresses emotion?
  – *Expressing emotions is important in life – not just on stage! Imagine what could happen if someone keeps emotions bottled up inside. What do you think might happen to that person over time?*

◆ What did you find most surprising about expressing emotion?
  – *Any answer is correct if it relates to what the student did and/or thought.*

End the lesson by saying, *In our next lesson, we will use just about everything we've learned so far. We will apply legato/staccato, choral speaking and moving, and emotional expression to explore how an actor creates a character!*

Archetype Pose

	One teacher doing all five Acts	Up to five teachers each doing one Act
When to do this lesson:	Rehearsals 31–40[16]	Rehearsals 7–8

Introduction

"Rebel", "Hero", "Advocate", "Pioneer", "Lover", "Gossip", and "Fool" are all words that remind us of types of characters in movies, plays, books, and perhaps our own lives. These one-word character descriptions immediately paint vivid portraits in the reader's mind and can be a useful way for actors to bring characters to life.

Imagine! What would Shakespeare's *Othello* be like without Iago as the archetypal Villain or *The Sorcerer's Stone* without Harry Potter as the adventurous Wizard? The Braggart incarnated by Bugs Bunny and The Glutton represented by Homer Simpson are current-day models, based on archetypes, that have amused us for centuries, long before animation or movies were invented.

Archetype is a universally recognized character often described in one word. The term stems from the ancient Greek root "arche", meaning "the first". "Type" means "to imprint/impress" or "pattern". Putting the two roots together to form the word "archetype" is a "first impression".

Archetypes are complex three-dimensional figures, whereas stereotypes are oversimplified one- or two-dimensional characters. See Table 5.8.3.

Table 5.8.3 Archetype and Stereotype Comparison

Archetype	Stereotype
An original concept, opinion, or image upon which others are based.	A conventional or oversimplified concept, opinion, or image.
Core impression on observers.	Surface impression on observers.
Comes from "within" the character and represents enduring attributes observed over time.	Comes from perceptions of character by observers of a single interaction or event.
Makes an impression on observers of a character's internal life such as desires and motivations.	Makes an impression based on opinions and ideas that preexist in the minds of observers and could have little to do with a character's internal life.

(Continued)

Table 5.8.3 (Continued)

Archetype	Stereotype
Stimulates deep thinking about a character's "back-story".	Discourages deep thinking about a character's "back-story".
Provides vocabulary to express and describe complex multi-faceted characters.	Provides vocabulary to express and describe simple one-sided characters.
Encourages students to consider characters as complex (made up of several archetypes in a story).	Encourages students to oversimplify characters (possessing a single attribute in a story).

Hamlet is an example of the "inner world" made visible by archetype and the "outer world" of stereotype as in:

Stereotype: (Spoiled) Rich Prince

vs.

Archetype: (Fighting) Avenger

Compare and contrast the character of Hamlet using the above descriptions. What comes to your mind? Which gets you thinking deeply about the character? The description, "spoiled rich prince" might paint the one-dimensional portrait in the reader's mind of a bratty young person of inherited wealth and compel the actor to play the role based only on that information. Students at PS6 in Manhattan, however, chose to play Hamlet as "The Avenger", fleshing out a three-dimensional portrait that activated their imaginations to wonder about what he might fight for, how he behaves, and what drives Hamlet's behavior. Rich discussions ensued about how *The Avenger* might restore his kingdom to order. Were we to settle with "spoiled rich prince" then most likely that's what we'll get on the stage with little to no understanding of what the character is thinking or feeling.

Actors assign, or make choices about, archetypes based on their interpretation of the character's actions and experiences and may embody different archetypes at different points in the story. In scene one, for example, Hamlet might be *The Victim* suffering from his mother's marriage to Claudius, *The Explorer* when the Ghost leads Hamlet away from the castle to inform Hamlet of the pernicious plot, and ultimately *The Avenger* who seeks revenge for the murder of his father. See Table 5.8.4.

> **Teaching Tip!**
>
> You or someone you know might have archetypes in the family: perhaps uncle Benny the Clown or your cousin Marie the Drama Queen.

Table 5.8.4 Archetype Examples

Angel (helps, supports, gives freely)
Beggar (begs, pleads)
Bully (provokes, insults, intimidates)
Champion (wins, competes)
Clown (entertains, jokes)
Cop (polices, regulates, controls)
Coward (runs, cowers)
Destroyer (destroys, annihilates)
Detective (investigates, inquires)
Engineer (designs, builds)
Father (nurtures, loves, protects)
Gambler (bets, risks)
General (commands, orders)
Guard (protects, blocks)
Glutton (consumes, eats excessively)
Healer (heals, cures)
Hermit (recluses, retreats)
Hero / Heroine (achieves boldly and bravely)
Hustler (swindles)
Judge (decides, balances)
King (rules, presides)
Lover (enjoys, relishes, devotes oneself)
Magician (conjures, mystifies)
Martyr (exaggerates personal difficulty, seeks sympathy or admiration)
Mediator (balances, negotiates, settles disputes)
Mentor (advises, guides, counsels)
Messiah (leads, saves)
Midas (creates wealth)
Miser (hoards, amasses)
Mother (nurtures, loves, protects)
Murder (kills)
Peacemaker (keeps peace, mediates)
Pioneer (explores, develops and creates new things)
Politician (maneuvers)
Provocateur (provokes, instigates)
Queen (rules, presides)
Rebel (revolts, objects)
Rescuer (rescues, saves)
Saboteur (sabotages, destroys)
Scribe (writes, records, documents)
Slave (serves, obeys)
Star (dazzles, shines, sparkles)
Student (learns, studies)
Teacher (instructs, teaches)
Thief (steals, takes)
Vampire (sucks, feeds)
Victim (suffers, contracts)
Warrior (fights, combats)
Wizard (mystifies, materializes)

Figure 5.2 Choral character team strikes the pose of The Avenger. (Illustration by Ian Dale.)

Exposing students to a range of archetypes will build an understanding that characters have a complex inner world. But how does that inner world reach an audience? It's invisible, isn't it?

Actors make their interpretation of the inner world visible to an audience not only by what they say and do but also through still pose – or what can sometimes be referred to as "body language". *The Avenger*, or any other archetype, becomes visible through a still position or shape of the body. But *how* does an actor strike a pose that reflects their interpretation of that inner world? See Figure 5.2 for an example of a choral character team striking the pose of *The Avenger*.

Clues to finding an archetype pose can be found in the prevailing actions of any given character because those actions reflect what the character wants or aims to accomplish at any given moment. *The Avenger*, for example, might want to punish or avenge. During rehearsal or in-class practice, the actor might explore these intentions through an aggressive, staccato gesture or movement that conveys the intention to punish or avenge. The ending position or shape of the body, which is held by the actor in stillness, is the resulting archetype pose that can be used on the stage. To put it another way, the actor moves their body to express the action and holds the resulting shape of the body. That still shape is the archetype pose that conveys the essence of *The Avenger*.

Archetype poses can be particularly helpful for student actors, especially if they are standing and listening on stage for long periods. The Chorus in Act 4 of *Hamlet*, for example, could strike poses of *The Reporter* (documents, informs), *The (Town) Crier* (shouts, pronounces), *The Coward* (runs, cowers), *The Cop* (polices, regulates, controls), or any other archetype inspired by the students' imaginations during or after speaking the line, "A rat, a rat! Hamlet in madness hath Polonius slain!"

This chapter explores how student actors convey their understanding of character archetype the same way an actor does: through a still pose. Sustaining a pose for a few seconds allows the actor to make an impression on the audience. Without still moments, the student's choices about a character could occur too quickly for the audience to see them.

Poses are everywhere in the world around us. Newspapers, magazines, and the Internet capture people in poses that convey information about who they are. Actors do the same thing every moment they're on stage. Even when still, actors express their understanding of the characters they play through pose.

Archetype Pose Lesson Plan

This activity helps students understand that poses grow out of the archetype they assign to a character. A pose, which is a still position or shape of the body, visually communicates information. On stage, they can help actors and audiences understand something basic about a character – its archetype or essence.

Students will:

◆ Learn that an archetype is a universally recognized character, often described in one word.
◆ Understand that pose is how an actor conveys information about their character through stillness.
◆ Know that pose is a character's stance in stillness.
◆ Be able to collaboratively decide on an archetype pose.
◆ Be able to pose in stillness as an archetype.
◆ Recognize a range of five or six archetypes presented as poses by their classmates.
◆ Respond critically to their classmates' ability to present their pose.
◆ Reflect on their experience to extend thinking.

For inquiry-based learning: turn your instructional aims into a question and write the question on the board prior to engaging students in the activity.

Throughout the lesson, encourage students to investigate possible responses to the question:

What information does a still pose convey to an audience?

Materials/Teacher Preparation

- ◆ One card per small group labeled with an archetype such as "Rebel", "Magician", and "Champion".
- ◆ Self-Assessment chart "Strike a Pose" written on poster board or the blackboard.
- ◆ Marker for tallying numbers.

Vocabulary

- ◆ **Archetype** (noun): A universally recognized character often described in one word.
- ◆ **Pose** 1. (noun): A still position or shape of the body. 2. (verb) To assume a position or shape of the body.
- ◆ **Cue** (noun): A signal to an actor to enter a scene or to begin, do, or say something.

> **Teaching Tip!**
>
> Referring to the students as "actors" during these activities often helps them develop pride in their work, a disciplined attitude about the art form, and self-esteem.

Step ONE: Jumping Off – Introduction and Vocabulary

1   In front of the class, stand silently and perfectly still in a neutral position. Then strike a pose that expresses the archetype of The Teacher. After five seconds return to a neutral position, and then strike a pose that communicates being The Student. Your pose could communicate studiousness or a thirst for knowledge – whatever you think will convey the essence of The Student.

2   Introduce the word *pose*, and ask students to use it in sentences to check for understanding. Ask students where they might see poses in their own lives and where they might use their body in stillness to express an idea they want to get across.

3   Ask students what they think poses do on stage. Why do actors take them? (Poses can help actors express something basic about a character, such as what a person might want or need out of life, for instance. A student might want to learn something, a teacher might want to instruct, and a bully might want to provoke). Link to

archetype by suggesting that these wants or needs remain invisible until the actor strikes a pose. Check for understanding by having a student or you strike a pose for a different archetype and have them identify what they believe the archetype is and what that archetype might want or need. Tell students that they will now work on expressing archetypes through poses in small groups.

Step TWO: Determining a Pose that Visually Expresses an Archetype

1   Break students into character teams of four or five.
2   Distribute one archetype card to each team.
3   Have students brainstorm for five minutes about what their archetype might want out of life. Ask, *What does this archetype want out of life?*
4   Have students collaborate and agree on one pose that everyone in the group will do to reflect the archetype. Coach, *Think about what still position or shape of the body will convey what the Rebel might do or want. See if you can imagine how your archetype might pose.*
5   Remind the students that:
    a   they should work together (listen to each other respectfully, respond to their peers) because you will look for evidence of collaboration when they share their work with the class;
    b   the criterion for assessment is everyone in the team holding the same pose for five seconds when they share their work with the class;
    c   to remain in line of sight of their audience of classmates;
    d   the activity has a structure:
        1   beginning (a neutral position)
        2   middle (moving into pose)
        3   end (holding the pose for five seconds)

Step THREE: Sharing Your Pose

1   Have students recall how you presented your pose, starting in a neutral position, moving into your pose, and then holding it for five seconds. Have each team share pose using the same presentation structure.
2   Explain that team members begin in a neutral position.
3   Have the audience of classmates give the action cue such as "3-2-1-ACTION!" to begin moving into the pose.
4   Keep time as actors hold the pose for at least five seconds and let them know when the time is up. Students may come back to a

neutral position at the end of their presentation.

5   Ask the audience of classmates, *What did you see? What did the shape of the actors' bodies convey? What kind of character or archetype do you think the pose represents?* Encourage discussion and diverse interpretations – all of which are correct as long as students can logically support their interpretation with what they saw. This is very important because asking students to think about their thinking[17] will deepen their learning!

> **Teaching Tip!**
>
> **Step THREE**
>
> This is an excellent opportunity to help your students understand that the audience doesn't always see and interpret things the way the students might want them to.
>
> Did the audience of classmates receive the information intended by the student actors who are sharing their work? Some side-coaching might be needed to help the actors make appropriate adjustments to their poses.

Step FOUR: Assessment of Pose Presentation

1   Remind the students that it is important for actors in theater to work together toward a common goal because without it there is no sense of ensemble and a feeling of the whole.

2   Ask the audience of classmates to look at the assessment you've written on the board and critique team by team with a show of hands whether all actors in each team sustained the same pose for five seconds (Table 5.8.5):

Table 5.8.5 Archetype Pose Assessment

	STRIKE A POSE			
	Poor (1) None	Fair (2) Some	Good (3) Most	Masterful (4) All
Sustained same pose for five seconds				

3   Begin with "Masterful" and ask the audience of classmates if they saw all actors in the team remain in the same pose for five seconds. Quickly count the number of responders and record that number in the appropriate box. Ask the audience of classmates why they responded the way they did for each team and what the team can do better next time. Continue asking the same question for each

team and filling in the score until all the teams have presented. Remind the students that this is not a competition but a process to help them learn how to critique each other's work while working together.

4   If students scored more ones and twos than they did threes and fours, it is a good idea to offer them another go at it. Remember that acting requires practice! The students should stick to the indicator of all members of their team sustaining stillness as a measure of success – not what they "liked" or "did not like".

5   Encourage feedback to the whole team instead of individual actors within the team. Keep the pace of assessment rapid and flowing.

Step FIVE: Reflection and Discussion

Lead a reflective discussion with the following questions (give students time to think about their responses)[18]:

- How does an actor convey information through stillness?
    - *Any answer is correct if it relates to what the student did, saw, and/or thought.*
- Did the poses presented today convey what the students were trying to communicate? Why or why not? How do you know?
    - *Any answer is correct if it relates to what the student did, saw, and/or thought.*
- Why do you think it is important for an actor to be able to pose in stillness as an archetype?
    - *If an actor's interpretation stays in their head, then the audience can't see it and may not understand what type of character they are playing or the character's wants or needs. Acting is about making the actor's imagination visible to an audience and pose is one example of that.*
- Why do you think it's important to pose for several seconds?
    - *Poses give the audience enough time to absorb the information the actor is conveying. If the information is important, then the actor might pose for a longer period. If the information is not important, the actor will not sustain a pose for very long if at all.*
- Where else do you see poses in everyday life? What do they tell you? Are those in daily life used for the same or different reasons?
    - *Poses are all around us and can be seen in pictures from newspapers, magazines, books, and on the Internet. Poses convey information about what a person might be doing and who they are "on the inside". What does a pose tell you about a person? How do you know?*

- ◆ What archetypes do you recognize in the school, your neighborhood, and on TV?
  - – *Harry Potter is sometimes The Explorer, The Magician, and others. Homer Simpson is most often The Glutton. A fictional character can be made of several archetypes throughout the life of a story. Archetypes on stage help mirror the complexity of real-life people and help us understand them.*
- ◆ What are the benefits of studying how an actor makes a character visible through pose?
  - – *Pose can make a stunning "core impression" on the audience and reveal who the character is "on the inside", which the audience needs to understand. Otherwise, the audience can become confused.*
- ◆ What did you find most surprising about posing to express an archetype?
  - – *Any answer is correct if it relates to what the student did and/or thought.*

Wrap up by sharing, *Next time, we're going to explore how meaning is conveyed in stillness using multiple characters in frozen pictures!*

Tableau Vivant Lesson Plan (with Focal Point Mini-Lesson)

	One teacher doing all five Acts	Up to five teachers each doing one Act
When to do this lesson:	Rehearsals 41–50[19]	Rehearsals 8–10

Introduction

This activity helps students understand how an actor conveys important moments in a play through still pictures as characters come into relationship with each other. On stage, tableaus can help actors and audiences understand the actions, relationships, and place of a scene.

Students will:

- ◆ Know that tableau vivant is a frozen moment presented on stage by actors who remain silent and motionless.
- ◆ Be able to collaboratively create a tableau vivant.
- ◆ Respond critically to their classmates' scenes in tableaux.
- ◆ Reflect on their experience to extend thinking.

For inquiry-based learning: turn your instructional aims into a question and write the question on the board prior to engaging students in the activity.

Throughout the lesson, encourage students to investigate possible responses to the question, which could be:

How are important moments in the play conveyed to an audience?

Table 5.8.6 *Hamlet* Scene Description Examples

Active verbs are **_bold italicized_** and focus the action

Act 1
King Claudius and Queen Gertrude **_toast_** their new marriage while Hamlet **_looks on_** in disapproval.

Act 2
The Players **_perform_** a murder scene for Hamlet, which gives him an idea.

Act 3
The Players **_reenact_** the death of the King as Claudius **_watches_** in horror. Hamlet and Horatio **_observe_** Claudius.

Act 4
Laertes and Gertrude **_watch_** in dismay as Ophelia **_sings_** a nonsense song.

Act 5
Hamlet and Laertes **_face off_** for a fencing bout. Claudius **_holds_** a cup of poisoned wine.

Materials/Teacher Preparation

◆ One card per small group labeled with a scene description between at least two characters from the play you are working on. See Table 5.8.6.

◆ Self-Assessment chart "Tableau Vivant" written on poster board or the blackboard.

◆ Marker for tallying numbers.

Vocabulary

◆ **Tableau vivant:** (noun phrase): A frozen moment presented on stage by actors who remain silent and motionless as if in a picture. (French: tableau: picture + vivant: living.)

◆ **Focal point**[20]: (noun phrase): Point at which the eyes are aimed.

Step ONE: Jumping Off – Introduction and Vocabulary

1 Show students a large photograph from current events with two or three characters. Without reading the caption, ask students to tell you what they think is happening in the picture. Ask them, *What do*

the poses tell you about each person's archetype? What do the characters seem to be doing? What is their relationship to each other? Where is each character looking and why are they looking in that direction? What verb might describe what each character is doing?

2   Ask students if they know why the saying "a picture is worth a thousand words" is so common. Introduce the phrase *tableau vivant* and ask students to describe a moment from their lives between at least two people that "froze" in their minds as an example.

3   Ask students how frozen pictures might be used in theater. Why might actors freeze at certain moments? (Tableaux convey information about characters' relationship to each other and to their surroundings. They are sustained to give the audience time to absorb the information.) Make the link to tableau by suggesting frozen pictures on stage are used similarly to the way photographs are used in newspapers, magazines, and on the Internet: to make a vivid impression about a moment by freezing it in time.

4   Turn students' attention back to the photograph and ask them to describe where each character's eyes are aimed. Introduce *focal point* as the spot at which characters' eyes are aimed. Ask them how the meaning of the picture might change if one of the characters were to change their focal point.

5   Tell students that they will now work in teams on a tableau vivant from the play they are working on.

Step TWO: Creating a Tableau Vivant that Freezes a Moment

1   Break students into teams of five or six.

2   Distribute one scene card to each team.

3   Have students brainstorm for ten minutes about how they could convey the meaning of their scene to an audience through a frozen picture. Coach:
   – *What still position or shape of the body will convey what your character is doing (his, her, or their action)?*
   – *How do the other characters in the scene affect your position or shape?*
   – *Where will you aim your eyes to convey the meaning in the scene?*

4   Remind the students that:
   a   they should work together (listen to each other respectfully, respond to their peers);
   b   the criterion for assessment is everyone in the team sustaining the same focal point for five seconds when they share their work with the class;
   c   several actors can play the same character but must agree on the same pose and focal point;

d   they should remain in line of sight of their audience of classmates;

e   the activity has a structure:
1   beginning (a neutral position)
2   middle (moving into tableau)
3   end (holding the tableau for five seconds) as you read aloud the scene card

> **Teaching Tip!**
>
> A tableau or scene can have a focal point of its own from the audience's perspective. If you are in the audience, where do your eyes go? That spot could be referred to as the "focal point" of the scene or tableau.

Step THREE: Sharing Your Tableau

1   Have students briefly recall the photograph and how it is a frozen moment. Remind them that the audience of classmates will need at least five seconds to absorb the information. Have each team share their tableaux vivant using the same presentation structure.

2   Explain that team members begin in a neutral position.

3   Have the audience of classmates give the action cue such as "3-2-1-ACTION!" to begin moving into the tableau.

4   Keep time as actors hold the tableau for at least five seconds[21] and let them know when the time is up. Students may come back to a neutral position at the end of their presentation.

5   Ask the audience of classmates, *What did the frozen picture tell you? What did the shape of the actors' bodies convey? How did focal point affect the meaning of the scene?* Encourage discussion and diverse interpretations – all of which are correct as long as students can logically support their interpretation with what they saw.

Step FOUR: Assessment of Tableau

1   Remind the students that it is important for actors in theater to work together toward a common goal because without it there is no sense of ensemble and a feeling of the whole.

2   Ask the audience to look at the assessment you've written on the board and critique team by team with a show of hands whether all actors in each team sustained the same focal point for five seconds (Table 5.8.7):

Table 5.8.7 Tableau Assessment

	Tableau			
	Poor (1) None	Fair (2) Some	Good (3) Most	Masterful (4) All
Sustained silent pose for five seconds				
Sustained focal point for five seconds				

3 Begin with "Masterful" and ask the audience of classmates if they saw all actors in the team sustain the same focal point for five seconds. Quickly count the number of responders and record that number in the appropriate box. Ask the audience of classmates why they responded the way they did for each team and what the team can do better next time. Continue asking the same question for each team and filling in the score until all the teams have presented. Remind the students that this is not a competition but a process to help them learn how to critique each other's work while working together.

4 If students scored more ones and twos than they did threes and fours, it is a good idea to offer them another go at it. Remember that acting requires practice. The students should stick to the indicator of all members of their team sustaining stillness as a measure of success – not what they "liked" or "did not like".

5 Encourage feedback to the whole team instead of individual actors within the team. Keep the pace of assessment rapid and flowing.

Step FIVE: Reflection and Discussion

Lead a reflective discussion with the following questions (give students time to think about their responses)[22]:

◆ How are important moments in the play conveyed to an audience?
 – *Any answer is correct if it relates to what the student did, saw, and/or thought.*
◆ Why is a picture worth a thousand words? How do you know?
 – *Any answer is correct if it relates to what the student did, saw, and/or thought.*

◆ Why do you think frozen pictures are used on stage?
  – *A still composition will allow an audience to absorb the visual informa-tion of a scene such as the character's archetype, how one character feels about another, or what the action of a particular scene might be.*
◆ Why do you think photographs are used in newspapers, magazines, and on the Internet?
  – *Photographs and still moments have enduring impact on an audience. Newspapers and magazines might use a photograph of war to convey the gruesome outcome of violence that facts described in words alone might not convey. The stage relies on the same idea: impressions on the audience are made through frozen images.*
◆ When you reflect on the day, what moments are frozen in your mind? What made the greatest impression on you today? Why?
  – *Any answer is correct if the student can say why.*
◆ What are the benefits to studying tableau vivant?
  – *Any answer is correct if the student can say why.*
◆ What did you find most surprising about creating a tableau vivant?
  – *Any answer is correct if it relates to what the student did and/or thought.*

Wrap up with something like, *As we practice our play, we're going to work together to choose important moments in the play to freeze in stillness for our audi-ence* like in Figure 5.3.

Figure 5.3 Students in tableau sharing the same focal points. (Illustration by Ian Dale.)

The Hamlet choral character team is looking at Laertes who is looking at Hamlet. Claudius is looking at Laertes in this tableau of one of the final scenes of the play.

Notes

1 Tableau vivant and focal point are combined into one lesson plan.
2 © 2003 Plank Road Publishing, Inc. All Rights Reserved. Used by permission. This link will take you to a musical example of legato/staccato to help support the concept. Permission was granted by the publisher of the song (Music K-8/Plank Road Publishing) for purchasers of this book to use the audio Sound Sample in conjunction with this lesson. (For the rights to perform the song or use it further in a classroom setting, the Performance Kit for "Legato Staccato" (SE-987) is available for purchase at www.musick8.com).
3 See "Wait-Time" in Chapter 8: Inquiry and Reflection.
4 If you are doing more than one Act, you might decide to do the acting lessons closer together. That's okay! Whatever works for you and your students is the best approach.
5 Piece of work: masterpiece of craftsmanship.
6 Faculties: abilities.
7 Express: exact.
8 Apprehension: power of understanding.
9 Quintessence: the purest form of something.
10 Quintessence of dust: dust in its finest form.
11 Professional actors rely on a line of dialogue or action that came before as a cue to begin. Students will be exposed to this idea during the rehearsal process.
12 If you are doing more than one Act, you might decide to do the acting lessons closer together. That's okay! Whatever works for you and your students is the best approach.
13 Colman A. *A Dictionary of Psychology* (3 ed.). Oxford University Press, 2008.
14 Corroborated during a phone conversation with Mrs. Plutchik in 2008.
15 Plutchik, Robert. Sixseconds "Plutchik's Wheel of Emotions: Exploring the Emotion Wheel". Web 29 December 2023. https://www.6seconds. org/2022/03/13/plutchik-wheel-emotions/—. Corroborated and clarified during a phone conversation with Mrs. Plutchik in 2008.
16 If you are doing more than one Act, you might decide to do the acting lessons closer together. That's okay! Whatever works for you and your students is the best approach.
17 Metacognition is the process of thinking about and monitoring one's own thinking and is an important higher-order process in theater, school, and in lifelong learning. See Chapter 8: Inquiry and Reflection for more information.

18 See "Wait-Time" in Chapter 8: Inquiry and Reflection.

19 If you are doing more than one Act, you might decide to do the acting lessons closer together. That's okay! Whatever works for you and your students is the best approach.

20 Focal point can also refer to the point in the "frozen picture" where the audience is looking. For now, we are encouraging students to become aware of the importance of where *they are aiming their eyes while on stage.*

21 Five seconds in silent stillness will feel like an eternity for students at this age. But encourage them to do the best they can because it's important for the audience to have time to take in the information.

22 See "Wait-Time" in Chapter 8: Inquiry and Reflection.

6

The Rehearsal Process

Introduction and Overview

Students will apply what they have learned from the acting lessons of Chapter 5 by rehearsing a forty-minute Shakespeare play culminating in a performance for the school community.

DOI: 10.4324/9781003489733-6

The rehearsal process requires patience and a vision of the bigger picture because it can be tempting to over-rehearse a moment or two to get it "perfect". This temptation should be avoided because theater-making is about practice and not about perfection. Mistakes will occur during the process and that is okay – it is part of what makes rehearsal.

There will be time to reflect on the lessons learned throughout rehearsals. For now, we will focus on:

◆ Staging students in movement pathways (blocking)
◆ Coaching students on their acting

Remaining focused on the above will help you stay sane while preparing for the culminating performance. Remember that this is an experience for the students to learn about Shakespeare and the fundamentals of theater. Their *acting* is the emphasis. Not the scenery, music, and choreography, which can be too much unless your school has a performing arts focus and access to appropriate resources to make them happen.

Because the play must be ready on time, the process will require that some artistic choices, such as how the actors move and speak, become a lesser priority than others as you prioritize movement pathways. You might be surprised, for example, that on the fifth day of rehearsal your students are not particularly audible even though volume and articulation were the subject of prior lessons. You might not have time to deal with it now. Do not be discouraged by that! Students require gentle coaching, reminders, and repetition throughout the process. Professional actors often need similar reminders.

Any great theater director knows how to prioritize just like great teachers. Have the courage to let some things go and remember that learning trumps dazzle. It is more important for students to learn about the play and how actors' artistic choices are impressed on an audience than it is to impress an audience.

Estimated time for one teacher to do all five Acts: When it comes to time, blocking forty minutes of Shakespeare is going to require a good deal of it. The process will need about 50 one-hour class periods to rehearse and block the whole forty-minute play if the play is going to be done by one classroom of students.

Estimated time for one teacher to do one Act: The process will require at least 10–12 one-hour class periods to rehearse and block one Act.

The above does not include time for:

◆ Shakespeare basics of Chapter 3
  – Ancillary information that is intended for teachers but may or may not be relevant for students

◆ Acting skills lessons of
   Chapter 5
   – Required for students.
     These lessons can be done
     concurrently during the
     rehearsal process
◆ Paraphrasing activities using
   the *In My Own Words*
   worksheets
   – Required for students
     but can be assigned as
     homework

See Teaching Tip! for a tip about
rehearsal time.

See Chapter 4 for more information.

> **Teaching Tip!**
>
> Underestimating rehearsal time is a common error in judgment when putting together school performances. If you don't have enough time for forty minutes, consider working with other teachers across a whole grade. Each teacher could take one Act to present the whole play in sequence!

Which Option Is for You?

Theater-making is an incredible way to build community within a school. It gets teachers talking to teachers, teachers talking to the principal and other staff, parents talking to you, and students talking to students.

As noted above, there are two recommended ways to stage it:

◆ With one teacher doing all five Acts
◆ With one teacher each taking one Act across a whole grade to present the whole play

If each teacher does one Act *across a whole grade of students*, then the amount of rehearsal time per class will be reduced because each of your colleagues could take one Act presented in sequential order at the culminating performance. That means each class would rehearse for up to twelve class periods instead of about fifty. Of course, it could be done in less time depending on how the pace of your rehearsals. If there are three classes across a grade instead of five, each class could get one Act and divvy up the remaining two Acts among the classes resulting in about nine or ten hours of rehearsal per class.

If you are new to staging it, then consider doing one Act. If you have more experience, then consider doing more. Each Act is interesting in and of itself, so don't put pressure on yourself to do more material than what is reasonable.

Rehearsal Cycle and Stages

Rehearsal is the process by which actors and a director block and practice a play. Over time, professional actors improve their performance by practicing artistic choices about speaking, moving, and stillness while receiving instructions from the director about movement pathways on the stage.

In your role as director, you are the "outside eye" for the student actors. The process can last up to four weeks or longer for a two-hour play in the professional theater.

No matter if you are doing one Act or more, at least three class periods each week are recommended for students to rehearse because students can forget the blocking if you wait much longer than that between rehearsals. The following stages of the rehearsal process will help to manage the expectations of the students, yourself, and the process.

To summarize the scope and sequence of Chapter 4:

Teaching Tip!

If students complain about their lines or the parts they are playing, advise them, *I am the director, and it's my job to ensure that the whole play comes off well. That means I need a similar number of students playing each character so the audience can hear the play. We will also need enough actors for each part if one or two of you are absent when we do the play.*

If You Are Doing All Five Acts

- ◆ **Beginning (rehearsals 1–20):**
    - Acting Lesson #1 Staccato/Legato Speech and Movement
    - Acting Lesson #2 Choral Speech and Movement
    - Read Aloud Acts 1 and 2 from Plot Synopsis[1]
    - Paraphrasing Worksheets for Acts 1 and 2 (homework)[1]
    - Block[2] Acts 1 and 2
        Teach and expect emergence in acting skills, especially:
    - Learning and understanding lines
    - Knowing acting areas
    - Blocking and notation
        Emergence of acting skills = meeting standard of knowledge or skill on cue *some* of the time.
- ◆ **Middle (rehearsals 21–40):**
    - Acting Lesson #3 Emotional Expression
    - Acting Lesson #4 Archetype Pose
    - Read Aloud Acts 3 and 4 from Plot Synopsis

- Paraphrasing Worksheets for Acts 3 and 4 (homework)
- Run through (review) blocking for Acts 1 and 2 before blocking Acts 3 and 4
- Block Acts 3 and 4

> Teach and expect emergence in acting skills, especially:

- Learning and understanding lines
- Moving as directed within acting areas
- Blocking and notation

> **Proficiency in** acting skills = meeting standard of knowledge or skill on cue *most* of the time.

◆ **End (rehearsals 41–50):**
- Acting Lesson #5 Tableau Vivant
- Acting Lesson #6 Focal Point
- Read Aloud Act 5 from Plot Synopsis
- Paraphrasing Worksheets for Act 5 (homework)
- Run through (review) blocking for Acts 3 and 4 before blocking Act 5
- Block Act 5

> Teach and expect emergence in acting skills, especially:

- Knowing lines
- Moving as directed within acting areas
- Blocking and notation

> **Mastery** of acting skills = meeting standard of knowledge or skill on cue *all* of the time.

> By rehearsal #50+:

- Run through (review) the whole play at least twice. Aim to do one run-through at the location of the culminating performance
- Actors should be off-book (lines learned) and not reliant on scripts for either lines or blocking notations

See Table 6.1.

If You Are Doing One Act

◆ **Beginning (rehearsals 1–3):**
- Acting Lesson #1 Staccato/Legato Speech and Movement
- Acting Lesson #2 Choral Speech and Movement
- Read Aloud your chosen Act from the Plot Synopsis[3]
- Paraphrasing Worksheets for 2/5 of your Act (homework)[3]
- Block[4] 2/5 of your chosen Act

> Teach and expect emergence in acting skills, especially:

- Learning and understanding lines
- Knowing acting areas

Table 6.1 Learning Lines Expectations Continuum One Classroom Doing All Five Acts

Rehearsals 1–15	16–30	31–45	46–50	50+
Emergent	Proficient	Masterful		
Few students in each team will know their lines and most will not when you block Acts 1 and 2. Coach them to glance at their scripts to catch small phrases then speak the lines in unison as they gesture. If possible, have students practice their lines and blocking at the same time – the movement will help them learn their lines!	About half of the students in each team should know their lines for Acts 1 and 2 and some of their lines from Acts 3 and 4. Repetition of blocking pathways is essential at this stage of the rehearsal process to assist students with learning their lines.	About 80% of students know their lines. While rehearsing: repeating tough spots with movement and speech as you cue the students. While at desks or transitioning to another place in the school such as the lunchroom or bus: run lines of one whole act cuing students and feeding lines as needed.	Stagger through all five Acts (whole play) Don't obsess over the lines. If 80% of students know most of their lines, you're good to go!	Culminating performance Course reflection

- Blocking and notation
    Emergence of acting skills = meeting standard of knowledge or skill on cue *some* of the time.
- ◆ **Middle (rehearsals 3–7):**
    - Acting Lesson #3 Emotional Expression
    - Acting Lesson #4 Archetype Pose
    - Paraphrasing Worksheets for 3/5 of Act (homework)
    - Run through (review) blocking from 2/5 of the Act before continuing to block your Act
    - Block 3/5 of your Act

        Teach and expect emergence in acting skills, especially:

    - Learning and understanding lines
    - Moving as directed within acting areas
    - Blocking and notation
        Proficiency in acting skills = meeting standard of knowledge or skill on cue *most* of the time.
- ◆ **End (rehearsals 7–10):**
    - Acting Lesson #5 Tableau Vivant
    - Acting Lesson #6 Focal Point
    - Paraphrasing Worksheets for the remainder of Act (homework)
    - Run through (review) blocking from 3/5 of the Act before continuing to block your Act
    - Block the remainder of the Act
    - Practice blocking of rough areas and run-through whole Act in the same location as the culminating performance

Teach and expect emergence in acting skills, especially:

- Knowing lines
- Moving as directed within acting areas
- Blocking and notation
    Mastery of acting skills = meeting standard of knowledge or skill on cue *all* of the time.

    By rehearsal #10+:

- Run through the whole Act at least twice. Aim to do one run-through at the location of the culminating performance
- Actors should be off-book (lines learned) and not reliant on scripts for either lines or blocking notations

See Table 6.2.

Table 6.2 Learning Lines Expectations Continuum One Classroom Doing One Act

Rehearsals 1–2	3–4	5–6	7–8	8–10
Few students in each choral character team will know their lines and most will not when you block Lines 1–12. Coach them to glance at their scripts to catch small phrases then speak the lines in unison as they gesture. If possible, have students practice their lines and blocking at the same time – the movement will help them learn their lines!	About half of the students in each team should know Lines 1–12 and some of Lines 13–25. Repetition of blocking pathways is essential to assist students with learning their lines.	At least 80% of students should have Lines 1–40 memorized. Coach lines of the Act while students move through blocking pathways. Repeat as needed until about 80% of students know their lines and cues.	At least 80% of students should know the remaining lines of the Act. Don't get too obsessed about lines memorization! It's about practice not perfection.	Coach students by repeating their blocking pathways, cuing entrances, and exits, especially for rough spots.

Casting in Choral Character Teams

Casting is one of the most important aspects of the rehearsal process. In this context, casting is the process of selecting multiple students to play the same character. Choral character teams are an idea borrowed from the ancient Greek tradition of the chorus, which enables the show to go on even if one or two actors are absent for the culminating performance. Working in a team can also be a safe place for students to take risks while providing the added benefit of increased audibility.

Any professional director will tell you that casting is a top priority because the choice of actor makes the director's interpretation visible to an audience. Casting is a directorial *choice*. Similarly to actors' artistic choices about speaking and moving, directors make choices about who is going to play each part based on their vision for the play. They do this by looking for the qualities, or capacity to embody them, of the characters to be played by the actors who are to play them. One director of *Hamlet*, for example, might want the title character to be introspective and melancholic and will cast an actor who can embody these ideas. Another director might see him as misogynistic in his treatment of Ophelia and Gertrude and cast a suitable actor. A director can require all these qualities and continue his search for an actor to embody all of them!

While professional directors aim for the right actor in the right part, directing in the classroom requires that everyone have a part to play. Otherwise, it's not fair. The process in the classroom is less about the qualities of individual students and more about fairly distributing the roles among the students available to play them to amplify the learning.

Fairness Strategies

◆ **Distribute lines equitably:** "You have more lines than I do!" says one student to another because of the developmental themes of fairness and justice that concern students at this age. Student perceptions run deep, and they will know if you are unjust, partial, or biased in the casting process and, as a result, could act out in unfavorable ways. The acting scripts for students have been designed to ensure ample opportunities for fairness. For example, longer passages of one choral character team could become a group chorus of the whole class, if desired. Even when the whole class isn't speaking at the same time, the scripts have several parts each in need of a competent team of students to play them.

- ◆ **Balance the *number* of actors in each team:** Equity in casting is increased if you divide the number of parts into the number of students and assign the students accordingly. If Act 1 has seven parts (including the chorus) and you have twenty-eight students, for example, then each choral character team should have about four students. If one or two teams have two or three characters, that's fine, but try to keep each team with roughly the same number of students. Once a student has been assigned to play a part then they should *commit to that part*. Otherwise, students could give up if the challenges escalate. Student actors need to learn to follow through and to make the character work, even if the going gets tough. If you are inconsistent, constantly changing your mind about who is going to play what part, then you risk destabilizing the equitable atmosphere of the classroom.

- ◆ **Balance the *personalities* in each team:** Some students are self-reliant and reserved. Others are gregarious and assertive. Some are leaders. Some are followers. Some will follow when playing Laertes, for example. Others will lead when playing Ophelia. When casting the class in teams remember to consider the:
  - – Introverts
  - – Extroverts
  - – Leaders
  - – Followers

  It would be unwise to cast a whole team of introverts to work together regardless of their intellectual abilities because acting is about *doing*. In theater, ideas are generated and then *enacted*. A whole team of introverts might struggle with, for example, who should say "3-2-1 ACTION" to begin, even though they might be very successful at generating ideas. The same holds for leaders and followers. A good mix of personalities in each team will encourage one individual to draw out the qualities of another.

- ◆ **Balance the reading levels:** Combine high-level readers with low-level readers and watch the magic begin! Rehearsing with high-level readers often draws the low-level readers out.

Sidecoaching

Viola Spolin describes sidecoaching as "free of authoritarian control, non directional; they are evocative, resourceful intimate whisperings, urgings, potentiators; stimulating, provoking, catalysts….To sidecoach effectively,

Table 6.3 Coaching Phrases per Acting Topic

Acting Topic	Possible Coach Phrases
Line of sight	*Can the audience see you? Adjust your position so you can be seen.*
Choral speaking and moving	*Move and speak together. Remember your cue so everyone in your team knows when to begin.*
Audibility	*I can't hear you from the audience. Articulate the consonants and speak at a louder volume.*
Expressing emotion through the face	*Keep your face in line of sight so the audience knows what you're feeling.*
Expressing emotion through the voice	*Radiate feeling through the voice – especially important if the audience can't see your face.*
Gesturing to express an action or intention	*Everyone in your team should begin and end together. This will help the audience understand your actions.*
Archetype pose	*Strike a comfortable pose when not speaking.*
Focal point	*If possible, choose a focal point so the audience can see your face.*
Tableau	*This is an important moment in the story. How many seconds did you decide to hold the still picture?*

use a simple, direct calling out". This approach is effective because it enables your students to receive feedback when it is most relevant. See Table 6.3 for some suggestions.

Learning Lines

As students use the paraphrasing worksheets, they will begin to learn more and more about what each line means. As they practice blocking pathways with you, gesturing and speaking their lines in unison with their peers, spoken lines will become more and more embedded in their bodies and memories. Later in the rehearsal process, most students should begin to be off-book (lines learned) for all their lines. This is a sensitive time in the rehearsal process, and there will be many stops and starts as you begin, stop, coach, and start again, stop, coach, and then take a couple of steps back, and then start again.

As you stagger through the process with students, encourage them to let go of carrying their scripts during rehearsals. Because they are working in teams, the other actors in that team might know the lines that other members forget – a relationship that will bolster the team. In cases where an entire team forgets a line, ask the students to follow this rehearsal protocol as you follow along in your script book ready to prompt the students. When actors forget a line:

1   They: call out "Line" while onstage and remain in a still pose.
2   You: read the line or its first few words to trigger actors' memories.
3   They: begin speaking and moving again.
4   Repeat as needed.

Eventually, most of the students will learn their lines as they practice blocking pathways. See Tables 6.1 and 6.2 for a sense of what to expect and when to expect it.

Some students will excel at learning lines and lead others. Others will follow the leaders and learn from them. Some will struggle through the whole process and not learn all their lines. So long as you see mastery of lines from roughly 80% toward the end of the rehearsal process, you'll be good to go. If not, some remediation suggestions include the following:

◆   Cue struggling students after school with the line that came before each forgotten line.
◆   Request that parents cue and run lines with their children at home.
◆   Request other choral character team members assist struggling students by cuing them and practicing the gestures and blocking.

> **Teaching Tip!**
>
> Memorization is developmentally appropriate, particularly for 10-year-olds. Don't let this age group give up too easily on that! Have students write their lines down; record them and listen to them; read and re-read them, etc. Most of all: practice!

You can expect *some* students to struggle with knowing all their lines even at the culminating performance. That's okay! It's much more important that students understand what they are saying, work cooperatively with their team, and learn about the play and perhaps a thing or two about Shakespeare. Don't obsess over the lines. Require what is realistic for about 80% of your class and let the cards fall where they may.

Understanding Lines: The Role of Paraphrasing Worksheets

Good actors understand what their lines mean. They will avail themselves of dictionaries to look up unknown words and, in the case of Shakespeare, even paraphrase his words in preparation for a role. *Student Paraphrasing Worksheets* are available separately for download and *Contemporary English Versions* for teachers are included within each Stage It play (see Chapter 9).

As homework or in a lesson preceding a particular rehearsal, students should use the *Worksheets* to paraphrase Shakespeare's words. That way, students will have the opportunity to study the meaning of their lines before rehearsing that section. You can check for understanding of vocabulary and comprehension during the rehearsal process and as you block the play. If students don't know what they are saying, then require that they spend additional time completing and studying their *Worksheets* after school. Consider requiring students to provide you with their completed *Worksheets* before that day's rehearsal so that you may check them against either the *Contemporary English Version* or your own paraphrase for understanding.

Stage Directions

...are pathways of the stage where actors move and stand. They are described from the actors' perspective. That means that stage right is to the actor's right as she faces the audience and stage left is to the actor's left as she faces the audience. Directors use these areas when instructing the actors as in, *Take two steps up stage right*.

Stage directions originate from the raked[5] stages of the European Renaissance of the 14th–17th centuries.

A raked stage enables the audience to see scenery and actors if they are at the back of the stage – upstage and away from the audience. Although most contemporary stages are flat, the originating vernacular has stuck and is used by professional theater artists today. See Figure 6.1.

Teaching Tip!

If you would like to demonstrate the concept of the raked stage in your classroom, take a book and:

1 Tilt it on the side
2 Roll a marble or pencil down it

Ask the students where they think "down stage" might be based on your demonstration.

UR = Up stage right   UC = Up stage center   UL = Up stage left
R = Stage right   C = Center stage   L = Stage left
DR = Down stage right   DC = Down stage center   DL = Down stage left

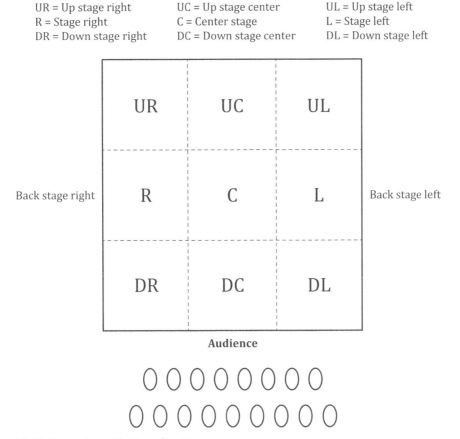

Figure 6.1 Bird's eye view with stage directions.

You can make use of stage directions in a small space in your classroom, the school auditorium, or any open space. Tape can be used on the floor to delineate a performance space, or you can just imagine the line between audience and actor.

Stage Blocking and Notation

Blocking refers to the pathways and positions on the stage that ensure actors can be seen. The term comes from an actor or an object "blocking" another actor who needs to be seen by the audience. In this case, the director of the play instructs the blocked actor to move to an area on the stage that allows line of sight.

For students at this age level, developmentally appropriate choices are those concerning how the characters speak and gesture. Making choices about blocking often exceeds the capacities of most students at this age (even for students ages 12 and 13) and in fact is not something most professional actors make choices about. For these reasons, the classroom teacher's role is to direct students from point A to point B with ample time for students to practice moving through those pathways. Keep in mind that what you might envision for a character portrayed by a single actor will need to be adjusted and simplified for choral character teams.

The goal of each rehearsal is to block about one-third (more or less) of each Act. When planning rehearsal time, it is important that enough time is allocated or you could wind up in an irreconcilable time crunch toward the end.

How do you block? Begin by informing students of your blocking

> **Teaching Tip!**
>
> Students don't always understand why they are being asked to move somewhere on the stage. Blocking is an excellent opportunity to engage in mini-reflections and lessons around line of sight, actions in the scene, etc. Ask, *Why do you think I asked you to move there?*

goal for the day. *Our goal for today*, for example, *is to block the Act through Hamlet's line "A little more than kin, and less than kind"*. Have students take their places on the stage by calling "places", and ask the students to read through a short section of the script to practice saying the words. Don't expect stellar acting as you instruct the actors when and where to move. Moving across pathways on stage is the focus for blocking and requires a good deal of concentration by the student. Coach emotions, audibility, line of sight, and other acting issues as you go through the process, but stay focused, for now, on blocking.

Rehearsals have a rapid and flowing pace and include the following feedback and practice procedure using a section of *Hamlet* as an example:

1   Place the students on stage by giving them instructions to go to specific acting areas. Direct, *King up center, Queen up left, Hamlet down left, Laertes down right, and Horatio down right of King and up left of Laertes,* for example.
2   Have students note in their scripts where they are standing for the beginning of each section of the script. They should write down in their scripts by whom or what they are standing beside or near.
3   Tell the actors where to go and on what line. Direct, *Laertes, take two steps left toward Hamlet after you hear Hamlet's line, "Readiness is all"*.
4   Wait until Laertes takes two steps left.
5   Have the Laertes team return to their starting position and try it again after you've given them their cue, which is Hamlet's line, *Readiness is all*.

6   Repeat the process two or three times until the students can get to their instructed position on cue.

7   Mini-reflect throughout by asking the students why they think they are moving there.

Teaching Tip!

Keep blocking simple! Often, the students' gestures and focal point can serve the purpose of conveying information to the audience without necessarily moving the characters across the stage.

The above rehearsal procedure will help your students get from point A to point B on the stage. At this point, you are like a traffic cop moving a class of student actors around the stage. It will be necessary for you and your students to note the blocking in the acting scripts,[6] which are included in each Stage It play. If you have a student or two who are good note-takers, consider asking them to be your stage manager, who is the person responsible for taking blocking notes in the professional theater.

How can you write it down? Each character can be represented on the page by an isosceles triangle with its apex as the focal point and an initial or other description such as "HR" for Horatio, "K" for King, "Q" for Queen, "L" for Laertes, and "H" for Hamlet as in Figure 6.2:

◆   **Laertes** has three actors in the team down right
    –   Noted as "L"
◆   **Horatio** has three actors in the team center right
    –   Noted as "HR"
◆   **King** has four actors in the team up center
    –   Noted as "K"

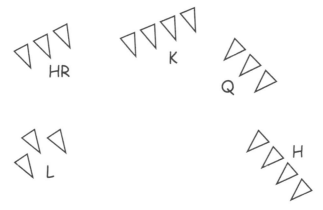

Figure 6.2 Bird's eye stage view single line formation.

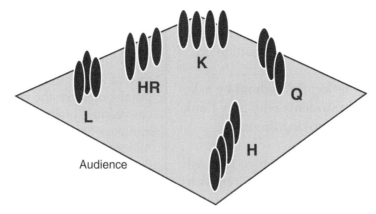

Figure 6.3 Audience view single line formation.

◆ **Queen** has three actors in the team up left
  – Noted as "Q"
◆ **Hamlet** has four actors in the team down left
  – Noted as "H"

Figure 6.3 illustrates how the above blocking notations would look on a classroom stage:

It is not essential for you to note how many actors are in each choral character team unless you want to. In that case, one triangle could represent one actor.

The formation in which actors are standing on the stage is also important. Alternatively to single-line formations in Figure 6.3, double-line staggered formations in Figure 6.4 could be an option assuming the tallest actors are in the rear. All but the Horatio actors are in a double-staggered line with the tallest actors behind the shorter ones.

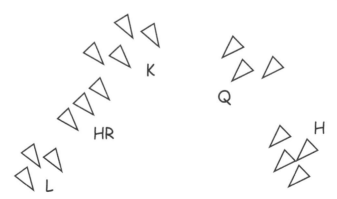

Figure 6.4 Bird's eye view staggered formations.

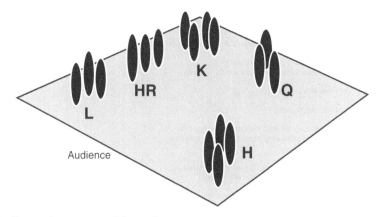

Figure 6.5 Audience view staggered formation.

Figure 6.5 illustrates how the above blocking notations would look on a classroom stage:

The members of the Horatio, King, and Queen teams are standing in all of the Figures so that students' faces can be seen. Note the *position* of the triangles in each of the teams in Figures 6.2 and 6.4. The apex of each triangle represents each character's approximate focal point.

It doesn't matter whether you choose single line or staggered formations (or something else entirely) so long as standing positions and blocking pathways reinforce students' understanding of line of sight to the audience. Coach students by asking if they are in line of sight and what they might do to adjust if they are hidden from the view of the audience. As noted earlier, students just like professional actors should note where they are standing in their scripts.

Blocking and other notes can be made in the acting scripts in the blank space to the right of the text as in Figure 6.6. Students make similar notations in their scripts. Don't worry if the scripts begin to look messy. A well-worn script is a tool of the trade and is evidence that it is getting a lot of use!

Stage Directions for Going from "Point A" to "Point B"

Sample stage directions to get students from "Point A" to "Point B" in Figure 6.6 are:

Places for start of Act 5 ("Point A"):

King up center (noted as "UC")
Queen up left (noted as "UL")
Hamlet down left (noted as "DL")
Laertes down right (noted as "DR")
Horatio down right of King and up left of Laertes
(noted as "DR of K and UL of L")

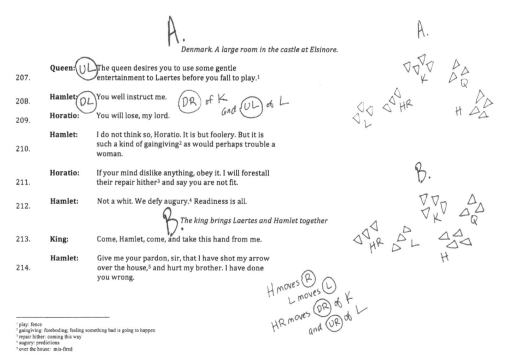

Figure 6.6 In-script blocking notation.

The cue to begin moving to the following positions ("Point B") is Hamlet's line 212 *Readiness is all*:

King remains up center and does not move
Queen remains up left and does not move
Hamlet moves one-step right (noted as "H moves R")
Laertes moves two or three-steps left (noted as "L moves L")
Horatio moves down right of King and up right of Laertes
(noted as "HR moves DR of K and UR of L")

After students arrive at "Point B", ask them if they are in line of sight of the audience. If not, ask them to self-adjust for line of sight and remember their ending positions ("Point B"). Go back to "Point A", give the cue line *Readiness is all*, and ask the students to repeat the movement pathways until about 80% have it correct. Then move on to the next section of the script. Remember to give students enough time to make blocking notes in their scripts.

Some blocking tips:

◆ Although line of sight to the audience is a top priority, sometimes actors will be blocked from audience view and you'll just have to live with that. It is not always possible to ensure 100% visibility with so many students.

◆ If actors' focal points are upstage, away from the audience, more volume will be required.

◆ If actors' focal points are downstage, toward the audience, actors' faces will be visible to the audience requiring that actors express appropriate emotion.

◆ Keep stage movement simple. Remember that even a step in the right direction can be dramatic.

Costumes, Props, and Scenery

… should be kept to a minimum and in some cases completely imaginary unless you have a good deal *more* time and resources at your disposal. Scenery and props require design and construction capabilities, which could involve additional courses of study. Stage It focuses on acting, which has been seen over time to be a developmentally appropriate area of focus for students at this age. Should you have a burning desire to involve costumes, props, and scenery, consider requesting that the visual arts teacher engage her students in the following inquiries so that students understand the meaning behind these physical elements of the play:

◆ **Costumes:** *What archetypal symbol best reflects the character?* For example, students at PS145, Brooklyn, decided that the witches of *Macbeth* were archetypal Prophets because they made so many predictions. They painted eyes on the cardboard cauldron and on masks to convey this information to the audience. *Hamlet* was portrayed as The Avenger represented by a sword at PS6, Manhattan. In all cases, the visual arts teacher provided direct instruction and activities that enabled students to create their symbols, which were adorned on either:
  – **Sashes:** worn across the body for all characters.
  – **Patches:** worn on the arm or chest.
  – **Character nametags:** worn around the neck with a piece of yarn or string.
  – **Headgear:** such as crowns for kings, helmets for guards, hoods for murderers, etc.

The following costume strategies have worked when a visual arts teacher was not available:

- **For a tragedy:** all black attire with character nametags around students' necks. If students have writing or images on a black t-shirt that would otherwise be acceptable, just have the student turn the t-shirt inside out.
- **For a comedy:** dress each choral character team in the same, brightly colored t-shirts with nametags around their necks.

◆ **Props:** *What object will best convey the action of the scene? What item will enhance the audience's understanding of the character? What object will best convey a sense of place or location for the audience?*

◆ **Scenery:** *Where does the Act or scene take place? What is the place in which the action occurs? What are the themes of the play and how can those themes be visually represented?* Students can paint, draw, and construct visual pieces that reflect their responses to these questions. Some examples:

- *Othello*: green eyes of jealousy
- *Julius Caesar*: murderous sword of deceit; hands of friendship
- *Hamlet*: avenging sword; coveted crown; loyal heart
- *Henry V*: the bow and arrow of noble victory

Teaching Tip!

Here is an example of a *Hamlet* costume breakdown used in Stages of Learning classrooms throughout New York City:

On the bottom:

All students: black or navy pants
Ophelia and Queen Gertrude: dark skirts

On the top:

King Claudius: large crown and red sash
Queen Gertrude: medium crown and red bow
Hamlet: smaller crown and red t-shirt
Horatio: yellow t-shirt
Chorus: multi-colored ribbon sashes
Ghost: tarnished crown and torn red sash
Laertes: blue t-shirt
Ophelia: wreath of flowers for hair and blue bow
Polonius: blue sash
Players: green ribbons at wrists, ankles, and neck; face paint

Images can be affixed to the back of the classroom, school auditorium, or wherever the culminating performance is to occur. Each Stage It play has more ideas about how to interpret it.

In all cases where costumes, props, and scenery are involved, aim to get the students to create them to deepen their understanding of the story. If you don't have time to engage in meaningful learning around these aspects of theater production, then omit them and focus on the acting. Students will leave the experience with a deep understanding of some material rather than little to no understanding of a lot.

Dress Rehearsal

Dress rehearsal should occur toward the end of the rehearsal process and:

- ◆ Integrate costumes, props, and scenery (if used)
- ◆ Practice the transition between each Act
- ◆ Practice the most challenging areas

The rehearsal should take place in the same location as the culminating performance because students, just like professional actors, can become disoriented and spatially confused if they

> **Teaching Tip!**
>
> This is a time when the process can get frustrating. Students might drop pencils while writing down their blocking; need a restroom break; or the fire drill could go off. Take deep breaths and try not to lose patience. Disruptions happen even in professional theater, and the dress rehearsal can sometimes be one big mess. That's part of the learning!

share their work with an audience in a space in which they have not had the opportunity to practice.

As earlier noted, the focus of the process for students should be on acting. The dress rehearsal will integrate basic costuming such as colored t-shirts, sashes, and character nametags if you have them. If you and your class are inclined toward more sophisticated production elements, then the students will need more time to practice with them.

Dress rehearsal can be hectic and stressful. Be cautious of becoming too demanding of the students because if you lose a feeling of ease then the collaborative atmosphere might be lost. Once that happens, it can be very challenging for student actors to do what is expected of them. Keep the positive energy flowing! Breathe. Have patience with the actors and *let them make*

Table 6.4 Double-Period Dress Rehearsal Rubric

Poor	Fair	Good	Excellent
1. No challenging areas are practiced.	1. Some challenging areas are practiced.	1. Most challenging areas are practiced.	1. All challenging areas are practiced.
2. Less than three Acts of the play have been practiced.	2. At least three Acts of the play have been practiced.	2. At least four Acts of the play have been practiced.·	2. All five Acts of the play have been practiced.
3. None of the students know transition cues and are in places when called.	3. Some students know transition cues and are in places when called.	3. Most students know transition cues and are in places when called.	3. All students know transition cues and are in places when called.
4. Less than three Acts have been practiced in the same location as the culminating performance.	4. At least three Acts have been practiced in the same location as the culminating performance.	4. At least four Acts have been practiced in the same location as the culminating performance.	4. All five Acts have been practiced in the same location as the culminating performance.
5. No costumes, props, and scenery (if applicable) are incorporated.	5. Some costumes, props, and scenery (if applicable) are incorporated.	5. Most costumes, props, and scenery (if applicable) are incorporated.	5. All costumes, props, and scenery (if applicable) are incorporated.

mistakes and find solutions themselves. They will learn more when an actor forgets a line and the other members of the team help him to recover than they will from chastisement.

See Table 6.4 for expectations about the dress rehearsal when minimal costumes, props, and scenery are used.

Time should be allowed at the beginning of the double-period dress rehearsal to share with students the structure of the activity. There will be some time at the end for their questions.

Dress Rehearsal Agenda

1   Rules of the performance space (ten minutes)
2   Practice challenging areas (fifteen to twenty minutes)

3 Stagger through the whole play focusing on the transition between Acts (eighty minutes) if you are doing more than one Act

4 Questions? (ten minutes)

The above dress rehearsal agenda is described point-by-point using *Hamlet* as an example:

1 **Rules:** After sharing the rehearsal agenda with the students, instruct them on the rules for the space such as:
   – Do not jump onto the stage
   – Enter and exit the stage from the appropriate places
   – Remain silent backstage
   – No gum-chewing
   – Disable electronic devices

2 **Practice challenging areas** one-by-one: If, for example, the Hamlet team's speech in Act 3 *To be, or not to be* needs to be practiced for audibility and the Chorus' entrance in Act 4 requires attention to blocking, then allow fifteen minutes in the beginning to work those two sections before proceeding.

   You will have to prioritize the challenges that can be reasonably addressed in the time you have. Although it could be tempting to practice more than the allotted time on challenging areas don't succumb! Forge ahead and focus on your top priorities.

   Even professional theater directors are tempted to polish moments in the play, but it is very important that students stagger through the whole play, calling for their lines when they forget, and acquiring the experience of flowing through troublesome spots even if something goes wrong.

3 **Stagger through the whole play focusing on the transition between Acts (if you are doing more than one Act):** Remind students that one of your goals for the activity is for them to get a sense of the whole play or Act, depending on what you have chosen to do. For that reason, you are not going to stop them very much, and they will have to keep going even if something goes wrong. Give an example of something that could go wrong such as someone forgetting a line or dropping a prop. Once students understand that they should keep going even if it's not perfect, advise them that you will stop the action at the end of each Act to practice the transitions between each Act. You will look for each student's ability to enter and exit the stage on cue after providing students with direct instruction about what those cues are. Advise students, for example:

Actors from Act 2 should be backstage and ready to enter upon hearing the Ghost's line, *Adieu, adieu, adieu, remember me* and actually enter on Hamlet's line, *So uncle, there you are, now to my word.* So: back stage actors have one cue to stand-by and one cue to actually enter. Actors already on stage who are also on stage for Act 2 will not actually exit the stage but will remain and move to their positions for Act 2. Any questions?

Call "places", give them an action cue such as "3-2-1-ACTION" or a line of text and allow the actors to stagger through the play as you look for understanding about entrances and exits. In Act 1, for example, once the actors speak *So uncle, there you are, now to my word*, the actors from Act 2 should already be entering as the actors from Act 1 are exiting. Have the students practice each transition until at least 80% of them have it right but remember you have about ten minutes to practice each transition. The clock is ticking so keep the pace rapid and flowing.

> **Teaching Tip!**
>
> If students are unsure about their entrances and exits, it's probably because they're confused about their cues, which are signals to do something. Be *specific* about when entrances and exits should occur by informing students of each cue for entering and exiting.

Transitions don't have to be dead space for actors and audiences. Narration can facilitate understanding for the audience and can be an appropriate role for the classroom teacher. You could write up a script for yourself to describe the essential action while the transition occurs. After Hamlet's last line of Act 1, for example, you could say something like:

> A ghost of a father appears and speaks of murder – his death so green! The clouds hang over the State of Denmark and the unhappy Hamlet whose sad father was murdered by the ambitious Uncle Claudius, who now wears the crown. Will Hamlet avenge this most foul act? How will he do it? Let's find out if he will be true to his father's demand in Act 2!

Figure 6.6.1 Sample narration for end of Act 1

Write your narrative script on note cards so you have them handy and be sure to identify each card by Act number in case they get out of sequence. This process is described further in Chapter 7.

4 **Questions?** Allow about ten minutes at the end of the dress rehearsal for you to give some last-minute advice to the players, answer questions, etc. The students will have questions following an intense period of rehearsal. If you don't build this time into your plan, it is likely to get sacrificed to needs that appear imminent. Even if you don't get to everything that you planned for the dress rehearsal, providing students with time to ask and respond to questions is vital to their understanding of the process. Consider, for example, discussing:

– *Are there transitions that are not working? Why or why not? What can be improved about them in the time we have left?*
– *How do basic props, costumes, and scenery change the experience for you? What do they convey to the audience?*
– *Who is coming to the culminating performance and how will they know about it?*
– *What would we like them to know about the play? About acting? About our interpretations?*
– *What concerns me as an actor right now? What can I do about it?*
– *What's my next step? What can I do to prepare for the culminating performance?*

Notes

1 Available separately for download.
2 block (noun): Pathways and positions on the stage that ensure actors can be seen.
3 Available separately for download.
4 block (noun): Pathways and positions on the stage that ensure actors can be seen.
5 A stage that is higher in the back than in the front.
6 The acting scripts for students available for download are ideally suited for noting blocking for actors and directors because each has blank space to the right of the scripted text.

7

The Culminating Performance

Introduction

It's show time! Just as in the professional theater, the first performance for an audience is resplendent with feelings as students rejoice in who is coming to see them, all the time and energy they've invested, and in their hopes to perform well, which of course includes remembering all of their lines and blocking.

It's pretty much the same for you. As their teacher and director, you've coached their acting skills, explored the meaning of Shakespeare's words,

DOI: 10.4324/9781003489733-7

and maybe even begged colleagues for extra rehearsal time in the school auditorium.

You and your students have come a long way, and now, more than ever, it's important to remember that the school performance is another learning opportunity with the following aims:

Students will:

◆ Perform their Shakespeare play to an audience of the school community
◆ Model for the audience key skills of the process

Audience will:

◆ Know about and experience one or two key skills of the process
◆ Understand the main plot points of your chosen play

The culminating performance doesn't have to be show and tell alone although there will be plenty of that going on. It can also engage the audience in learning about this course of study in Shakespeare and drama through the following five steps:

Welcome the audience

Introduce them to what they're going to see and hear

Provide direct instruction and student modeling of key concepts

Present the play with narration

End the experience

The Audience

Who is your audience? That is the question! Whether it is another class or grade in the school, parents and family members, or a local community center, the performance should be suited to the aims you have for your students, and it is advisable to engage them in the process of determining who the audience will be.

Possible audiences could include:

◆ Another class or classes in the same grade
◆ Another class or classes in an earlier grade
◆ A whole grade
◆ Parents
◆ Local businesses
◆ Community center
◆ Senior center

While parents are the likely choices, also think about others in the community who might derive benefit or contribute something meaningful to the community-building aspect of the experience such as:

◆ Photocopying of the performance program
◆ Food for a post-show potluck
◆ Neighborhood public relations and marketing
◆ Adults with theater experience who have acted in Shakespeare's plays and will facilitate a post-show discussion

Once you and your students have decided on a suitable audience, now you'll have to get the word out. Some marketing possibilities include:

◆ E-mail to parents and family members
◆ Letters home
◆ Posters around the school
◆ Announcements on social media, in local newspapers, newsletters, and community calendars

If the culminating performance will be out-of-doors, rain or other inclement weather could be a possibility. Check the weather report in advance! At the Carrie E. Tompkins Elementary school in Croton, New York, students presented *Macbeth* to an amusing murmur from the audience as the Banquo team looked skyward and said, *It will be rain tonight.* It was a good thing most of the audience brought umbrellas because these enthusiastic students would not have considered a postponement. It was they who insisted that the show must go on. Even in the rain!

It will be up to you and your students to decide who the audience will be and what information they will need to enjoy the experience. By now, you and your students have become experts on the play, but the audience might not be as far along.

Audience Program

An audience program in the school context is often a one- or two-page document photocopied back-to-back containing the essential information about the presentation such as:

- ◆ Name of the play
- ◆ Date, time, and location of the performance
- ◆ Your name
- ◆ Your students' names and their roles
- ◆ "Thank you" to people who contributed to the process

Space permitting, theater programs are also opportunities to:

- ◆ Briefly describe the plot
- ◆ Briefly describe the aims for this course of study in drama and Shakespeare
- ◆ Announce upcoming activities at the school
- ◆ Recognize community members for contributions to the school or presentation

Although programs can make meaningful mementos for students, sometimes programs are not supplied at all. These days, they can even be created digitally. It is up to you since they will require more of your time. See Chapter 9 for a time-saving template!

Prepping the Performance Space and House

Before opening the "house", which is what the auditorium is called in professional theater, it should be prepared appropriately for your audience. The "house" could also refer to the audience seating area for outside performances. It is important to run through the play at least two times in the performance space before presenting publicly. Otherwise, students can become disoriented and confused in the new space.

Following are two checklists: one for the performance space and one for the house where the audience sits. If you've engaged a student as a stage manager who might not be inclined to take on an acting role, this is an excellent role for them:

Checklist for the performance space:

- ❏ Clean the floor and check for any dangerous items such as nails, excessive slippery surface, etc.
- ❏ Clear objects from the stage except for any scenic items you might require.
- ❏ Practice opening and closing the curtains if you are going to use them. If not, just leave them open.
- ❏ If presenting outdoors, check the weather report and come up with an inclement weather plan (will the presentation go on no matter what or will there be an alternate date and location?).

Checklist for the house:

- ❏ Ensure general tidiness: Pick up litter, clean soiled chairs, etc.
- ❏ Adjust temperature if possible: Remember that it will get warmer in the auditorium if there are a lot of people inside. Adjust the temperature to about 70° if you can.
- ❏ Remove obstructions to line of sight if possible: If the item is movable, such as a three-legged stool or microphone stand, remove it from the line of sight of the audience if it does not play a role in your presentation.
- ❏ Engage ushers: Volunteers, students, and even parents can often help to manage the crowd. It can be helpful to enlist the help of a couple of people to assist with answering questions about restrooms, length of the play, etc. Generally, and unless your school follows protocols, the audience will be able to find their seats without assistance. The ushers' role for school performances is more about information sharing.
- ❏ Consider disability options: Some members of your community might require access through pathways that are wide enough and clear of obstructions. 42" of clearance is wide enough for most wheelchairs to pass. Since people in wheelchairs always bring their own chairs, it won't be necessary to provide them with seating unless they request it, but it will be necessary to ensure an open pathway to an area with an unobstructed line of sight. Consider assigning one or two ushers who are responsible for disability access and reserving some seats in the front for people who are hard of hearing or deaf.

❏ Rules, which can be posted on a sign, printed in the program, or orally shared before the performance:
  – Food or drink is not allowed in the audience. This can be distracting to the student actors.
  – Mute mobile communication devices. Ringing phones are too distracting for students.
  – Photographs and videos are permissible, but cameras with flashes are discouraged.
  – No talking. Ditto on the distraction.
❏ For outdoor presentations, be sure to make it explicit on the invitations or other marketing materials that the performance is outside and advise audience members accordingly. Will seating be provided, for example, if the presentation takes place in a park? Will there be an option to sit on the floor? If so, suggest the audience bring a blanket.
❏ Consider blocking off some rows in the house for students to sit in pre- and post-performance. You can use tape or signs taped to chairs for this purpose. Don't forget! Students will need a place to hang out before performing. If several classes across a whole grade are involved, think about where the entering classes will be and where the exiting classes will go.

Audience Take-a-Ways

You and your students may know more about Shakespeare than the audience at this point because you have been studying and practicing for a while. Consideration of what you want the audience to know and understand about this experience will extend the learning into the community.

Brainstorm with students what they think the audience should:

◆ **Know** about the process: What skills, strategies, and processes do they consider essential to acting? What have they learned about Shakespeare that they would most like to make explicit for the audience? What do they think the audience must know to derive the most from this experience? Is it important, for example, that the audience knows why you are using choral character teams? Why was that choice made? Are there any fun facts or notable quotes you'd like them to listen for?
◆ **Understand** about the process: Should the audience understand why you chose this particular play? What are its themes? Why do they

think it has endured for hundreds of years? What does the audience need to understand about acting? Is acting as easy as it looks?

◆ **Do** as their next step: What should they do at home? At the school? Where can parents or community members learn more about this play? Are their local theater companies presenting the play?

Exploring a few learner outcomes for the audience will actively engage the community in experiential learning and provide the necessary background information to facilitate…

Direct Instruction and Student Modeling

Once you've determined what you would like the audience to know, understand, and do then you can determine how to achieve it. Stages of Learning has seen success with three instructional strategies for the audience including:

◆ **Direct instruction:** Just as you would for your students, provide the audience with instruction about what they are about to see and things to listen and watch for as a basis for what is to come. If you and your students, for example, have decided that one of the things you want the audience to know is that staccato and legato movement and speech are two artistic choices that can be made by the actor to convey different meanings, then provide your audience with that information and ask them to watch and listen for different meanings during the presentation. Audience members could listen for how the students have chosen to speak two of the famous lines of the play, for example: *To thine own self be true* and *Neither a borrower nor a lender be.*

◆ **Student modeling:** After you provide direct instruction, then have several of your students model the concept for the audience. Request that the audience repeat what the students have done. The audience can do it from their chairs or in whatever way they are most able. If, for example, the students have demonstrated choral speaking and one of the most important lines in the play is *To be or not to be, that is the question*, then have the audience repeat that line in unison after receiving some direct instruction from you and modeling from your students. Do enough modeling to get the big ideas across and spend no more than ten minutes doing this. Otherwise, you run the risk of deflating your actors who are standing by backstage.

◆ **Inquiry:** Perhaps in the program or as a verbal component of intro-
ductory narration, ask the audience essential questions such as:
  – How do actors convey understanding of their characters to an
    audience?
  – (For *Hamlet*): What is rotten in the state of Denmark and why?
  – (For *Julius Caesar*): Why is Caesar betrayed and murdered?
  – (For *Othello*): Why does Desdemona die?
  – (For *Henry V*): Why is King Henry successful at Agincourt even
    though he was outnumbered five to one?

The above instructional strategies have been shown to effectively engage
audiences as well as actors in experiencing culminating performances as
active learners.

Narration

The previous chapter introduced narration during the dress rehearsal as a
transitional bridge from Act to Act. This section explores narration in greater
detail. For the audience, narration can facilitate their understanding of the
play and can be an appropriate role for the classroom teacher, parent, or other
eager adult. For the students, it gives them the necessary time to move from
backstage to on-stage positions.

The narrator is, in effect, the Master of Ceremonies. Modeling audibility
for the students, using gestures, facial expressions, and other acting skills,
will grab the attention of the audience. But the presentation will need one
more thing to do that: some sort of sound or signal that the show is about to
begin: a drum or other musical instrument, flicker of lights, or sound effect.
Stages of Learning teaching artist used Tibetan Singing Bowls to successfully
manage the crowd and get their attention.

Once you have the attention of the audience, it is time for the Act transitions. As noted in the previous chapter, after Hamlet's last line of Act 1, for
example, the narrator could say something like Figures 7.1 and 7.2.

A ghost of a father appears and speaks of murder – his death so green! The
clouds hang over the State of Denmark and the unhappy Hamlet whose
sad father was murdered by the ambitious Uncle Claudius, who now
wears the crown. Will Hamlet avenge this most foul act? How will he do
it? Let's find out if he will be true to his father's demand in Act 2!

Figure 7.1 Sample narration for end of Act 1.

An example for the end of Act 2:

Hamlet's trap is set! The traveling actors will act out a play for the King after receiving some additional lines from Hamlet. While it is words that Hamlet reads in Act 2, it will be the face of the King that Hamlet will read in Act 3 as the King hears a play about a murder and winning a dead man's wife. Let's find out if the play does indeed catch the conscience of the king!

Figure 7.2 Sample narration for end of Act 2.

Write the narration script on note cards or mobile devices small enough to slip into a pocket and identify each card by Act number in case they get out of sequence.

The End

Congratulations! You and your students have presented, now what? The actors have bowed, and the audience is clapping. Do you just let it be or is something else needed? Sometimes final words, unless they're Shakespeare's, can deaden the spirit of the play and almost always be extraneous. If you, your principal, or some other colleague *must* say something, celebrate with the students for a few moments and then instruct them to get comfortable to hear what is to come. Otherwise, consider saying something to the audience like *Thank you for coming and please let me know if you have any questions or thoughts about what you've experienced here today.* Then let the enthusiasm of the experience resonate with the audience. Everyone will need to let off a bit of steam – even you! There will be time to reflect later – a process that could even involve social media (see Teaching Tip!).

Teaching Tip!

Consider creating a Facebook page for the culminating performance where the school community can post pictures, videos, comments, and questions.

See Chapter 9 for a student certificate to share with students after the performance or course-end reflection.

8

Inquiry and Reflection[1]

DOI: 10.4324/9781003489733-8

Introduction

The wonderful world of theater-making for elementary and middle school students involves acting, rehearsing, and culminating performances. In so doing, students acquire experience that can resonate for years to come. However, doing it alone is not enough for students to make meaning of the experience.

Building understanding of theater-making processes for students is supported when they:

◆ Use theater vocabulary
◆ Express understanding through language that describes relationship similarity
◆ Ask penetrating questions prior to and during an art-making experience as a framework for performance assessment
◆ Ask reflective questions during and after an arts experience to encourage critical thinking
◆ Ask questions whenever they want about issues they care about to make connections and generate ideas
◆ Wait in the sacred sometimes awkward space of silence to think after a question has been posited

Facilitated opportunities for inquiry and reflection amplify a potentially exhilarating emotional experience by helping students make meaningful cognitive connections. The student actor might relish Hamlet's indecisiveness, Othello's naiveté, Brutus' brutality, or Henry V's heroism. But has she generated ideas and questions that enable her to investigate why the characters behave the way they do? Has she connected meaningfully enough to share *her* interpretation with an audience and not just a well-intended teacher's directorial vision? Does she understand why she chose to speak or move in a certain way?

Inquiry and reflection galvanize curiosity that leads directly to critical thinking because questions are both specific and generative. These processes endow students with implicit authority to make their own choices about acting a role. If, for no other reason, because they have thought deeply about it. This chapter aims to make the case for inquiry and reflection in your classroom by:

◆ Describing the reflective practices used in Stages of Learning classrooms
◆ Exploring topics for further study, if desired
◆ Encouraging frequent inquiry and reflection with students

Spotlight on Learning

Learners reflect, self-regulate,[2] and inquire. Self-reflective teachers, students, artists, and other learners examine their experiences, inquire about effectiveness, and draw conclusions that influence subsequent learning efforts. "Ideally, self-reflective practice allows students to assess their own learning progress and the effectiveness of strategies, alter their approach as needed, and make adjustments to environmental and social factors to establish a setting highly conducive to learning".[3]

Inquiry and reflection are cyclical interdependent processes that enable rich and relevant connections to enable learning. Learning, by definition, requires that such connections be made. Without inquiry and reflection, students can put on one helluva show but not understand what it means.

Professional actors and artists, too, can perform a character without necessarily understanding why they do the things they do. Competency for a professional actor involves, among other things, their ability to move appropriately in costume, which could appear to be a hundred or a thousand years old. Costumes might involve corsets, even for men, and while the actor must know how to move while costumed his lack of knowledge about the attire most likely will go unnoticed by the audience so long as he moves effectively while wearing it. Since many professional actors do not receive their costumes until the dress rehearsal, only the most curious among them will inquire into and learn about their silhouette, choices of fabric, and design inspiration. For Broadway actors who replace other actors, fitting the costume is essential. It doesn't matter to most producers if the actor understands the costume design so long as he fits into it.

An actor's lack of understanding may not be limited to costumes.[4] Sometimes the societal context in which the story takes place can be elusive. Shirley MacLaine is a brilliant actor who illustrates this point. She noted over thirty years after she made *The Children's Hour*, a movie based on the play of the same name about a vindictive child who begins a rumor about two women in a lesbian affair that results in the closing of the school, "We were in the mindset of not understanding what we were doing".[5]

Why does this happen? Professional actors focus on conveying individual artistic choices about the characters they play in the context of a director's vision. For students, performing or thinking only about individual characters would be learning opportunities lost because there is far more to a play than just the actor's part. Even if students understand audibility enough to be heard ten rows into the auditorium, the meaning behind the lines themselves could be lost if not for some reflection:

> …which, applied to the act of learning, challenges students to use critical thinking to examine presented information, question its validity, and draw conclusions based on the resulting ideas. This ongoing process allows the students to narrow possible solutions and eventually form a conclusion. The result of this struggle is achieving a better understanding of the concept. Without reflection, learning ends "well short of the re-organization of thinking that 'deep' learning requires" (Ewell 9). Effective learning situations require time for thinking. Students also reflect on themselves as learners when they evaluate the thinking processes they used to determine which strategies worked best. They can then apply that information about how they learn as they approach learning in the future.[6]

Simply put, reflection is looking back on what students think they have done to determine what they think they learned from it. Notice the repetition of the word *think* in that sentence. Shakespeare repeats something when he wants us to relish it. The same is true here. The word *think* or *thinking* appears in Shakespeare's full-length *Hamlet* fifty-three times. Shakespeare thought it was important and so should we when theater-making with students.

Research has shown that children can be taught reflective strategies, including the ability to explain to oneself to improve understanding, note comprehension challenges, predict outcomes, activate background knowledge, plan ahead, and apportion time and memory.[7] Throughout these processes, questions are likely to be asked of oneself, about the process, and of others. Embedded in reflective practice is the continual engagement of questions – or *inquiry*.

"If you envisioned images of children actively posing questions, seeking answers to questions that they care about, demonstrating a strong interest in outcomes, and discussing their theories and ideas with others, you've shared in a glimpse of what makes educators so excited about the possibilities of inquiry-based learning".[8] According to Grotzer, inquiry requires an environment that supports risk-taking. This means that:

◆ Question asking is invited
◆ "Mistakes" are valued for the learning they provide and as natural parts of the inquiry process
◆ Open-ended questions are asked and appreciated

- ◆ There's more than one possible answer
- ◆ Theorizing and considering evidence is considered more important than a "right answer"
- ◆ Sometimes questions are asked but not answered
- ◆ All ideas are okay to share
- ◆ Ideas are discussed for their explanatory potential, ability to solve the problem, and so on, as opposed to being called "good" or "bad", "right" or "wrong"[9]

In your role as theater director, the above points might feel like they encumber the process of putting on a school play, particularly if a strong directorial vision prevails. Learning goals for students should supersede directorial vision in a school environment, however, because of the potential lessons learned from making those choices. Balance between a teacher's directorial vision for the play and student's thinking about it, inquiring into the play's meaning, artistic choices made by the student actors, self-regulating and adjusting, and planning future courses of action can generate a rich and rewarding field of learning.

Metacognition

Metacognition is a dense word and understanding it can be elusive and confusing. Its five syllables twist tongues and minds as educators wrap their brains around it. Hamlet might like the word for reasons other than twisting tongues! In one scene, Hamlet says he will take his revenge, and in a later scene, he realizes he cannot commit murder. What got in his way? Only *thinking* made it so. This Prince of Metacognition might be called a master of self-regulation.

Metacognition *is the process by which learners think about, monitor, and regulate their own learning.*[10] While Hamlet's thinking is often spoken aloud, metacognition is often an internal dialogue with oneself.

Like Hamlet, students can be engaged in internal and external thinking dialogues through facilitated conversations, or reflections, at different times during the theater-making process.

Kinds of Reflection

There were three kinds of reflection used at Stages of Learning. They are distinguished by when they occur and their duration:

- ◆ **Mini:** Occur frequently, are relatively brief, and embedded in the direct instruction, mini-lesson, or activity. Mini reflections are always welcome but essential when you see puzzled looks on (roughly) 20% of the students. Example:

- – Students have been instructed about conveying emotion through the voice by modeling *To be or not to be that is the question* with emotion and without. Teaching artists or classroom teachers might ask, *What are you hearing? Which one is better? Why do you think that?* followed by some wait-time for students to respond and then practice for themselves.

◆ **End-of-lesson:** Occurs at the end of each forty-five-minute lesson and is between five and ten minutes in duration.
- – That day's lesson on stillness could be followed by asking, *How does an actor convey information through stillness? Why is stillness important in theater? What do you think it means to the audience if a scene was held still for one second? Five seconds? Ten seconds? What does the length of time a scene is held in stillness do for an audience?*

◆ **End-of-course:** Occurs at the end of the course of study for one whole class period. An example is the final topic of this chapter.

Kinds of Questions

There are two broad categories of questions: high inquiry and low inquiry. High-inquiry questions are open-ended and encourage divergent thinking. Low-inquiry questions tend to require yes or no responses and converge toward one correct response.

Jack Hassard compares and contrasts high- and low-inquiry questions: "Low inquiry questions tend to reinforce 'correct' answers, or focus on specific acceptable answers, whereas high-inquiry questions stimulate a broader range of responses, and tend to stimulate high levels of thinking. There is evidence to support the use of both types of questions. Low inquiry questions will help sharpen students' ability to recall experiences and events....Low inquiry questions are useful if you are interested in having students focus on the details of the content of a chapter in their textbook".[11] See Table 8.2.

There is a role for both kinds of questions in the classroom. Checking for understanding of a vocabulary word could rely on a low-inquiry question. Asking students to self-assess with support of their claims will require a high-inquiry question. Practically speaking, both kinds of questions are needed in teaching and learning, and it is often true that a simple empirical observation can yield the most generative and open-ended questions and insights.

Relationship to Assessment

Assessment in Stages of Learning classrooms helped to answer the question *How well did student actors perform a particular skill?*

Teaching artists embedded opportunities for students to assess their classmates following peer presentations in each classroom at some point in each lesson. Teams of student actors present their work in choral character presentations to the remainder of the class, who rate them using scales such as in Table 8.1.

Table 8.1 Stillness Assessment

	Stillness			
	Poor (1) **None**	**Fair (2)** **Some**	**Good (3)** **Most**	**Masterful (4)** **All**
Sustained pose for five seconds at end of scene				

Table 8.2 High-Inquiry and Low-Inquiry Characteristics[12]

High Inquiry	**Low Inquiry**
Perform an abstract operation, such as multiplying, substituting, or simplifying.	Elicit the meaning of a term.
Rate some entity as to its value, dependability, importance, or sufficiency with a defense of the rating.	Represent something by a word or a phrase.
Find similarities or differences in the qualities of two or more entities utilizing criteria defined by the student.	Supply an example of something.
Make a prediction that is the result of some stated condition, state, operation, object, or substance.	Make statements of issues, steps in a procedure, rules, conclusions, ideas, and beliefs that have previously been made.
Make inferences to account for the occurrence of something (how or why it occurred).	Supply a summary or a review that was previously said or provided.
	Provide a specific, predictable answer to a question.

Because students present their work in choral character teams, a device borrowed from the ancient Greek chorus with added benefits of audibility and multiple casting in case of the inevitable absences on performance day, the variable along the scale from one to four is *quantity* of students in each team, as in:

- Masterful (4): *All* members of the team demonstrate the skill.
- Good (3): *Most* members of the team demonstrate the skill.
- Fair (2): *Some* members of the team demonstrate the skill.
- Poor (1): *None* of the team members demonstrate the skill.

Stages of Learning students were in grades 3–8, and assessment was a serious and literal undertaking for many of them, particularly in grades 3–6. Students would, for example, count on their fingers how long presenting classmates remained still. Some students could sustain a pose for five seconds and some couldn't. Ultimately, students knew that assessment was embedded in each lesson and sometimes were even given a second or third try after hearing feedback from their classmates. The teaching artist and classroom teachers would ask questions to get the students thinking about and defending their feedback (as audience) and performance (as actors).

The inquiry *How well did we perform as actors?* drove the quantitative assessment by the students, but the ensuing conversations about that criterion, in this case still pose, was predicated on peer observation. The inquiry and its accompanying assessment were a turnkey into rich, complex, discussions around issues of stillness, body language, important moments in the play, and time required for messages to get across to the audience.

Classroom assessment was more formative than summative, served as a mirror about the quality of that day's instruction, and was in constant interplay with reflective conversations.

What to Listen for While Asking Questions

Reflective practice can coax visible and audible indicators of learning, such as:

- **Correct use of vocabulary:** Students use theater or Shakespearean vocabulary taught during the course of study as in, *Floyd was five minutes late to class today. A plague upon thy house!*[13]

◆ **Stories about transfer of knowledge:** Students describe moments or demonstrate behaviors in which they extended what they have learned in one context to a new context. Examples of indicators:
  – Line of sight: Students self-adjust to be seen by the audience when presenting to a community group.
  – Audibility: Students increase volume without instruction when addressing the PTA about the importance of theater instruction.
  – Character: Students recognize an archetype they have studied in images or descriptions from books, the Internet, and other sources and can tell you what they see in the image that makes them see similar features.
◆ **Analogical reasoning** is learning by comparison. Specific language to listen for includes comparisons, metaphors, similes, allegories, and parables. It involves transferring knowledge from one experience or known system to another (e.g., humans have hearts, therefore rabbits have hearts)[14] and "can be employed between any two items that belong to the same fundamental category".[15]

Stella Vosniadou defines analogical reasoning "as the process of identification and transfer of a relational structure from a known system (the source) to a less known system (the target). This process is more general than metaphor and can apply even between systems that belong to the same category".[16] It is both the cognitive process of comparing information from a similar content domain to another particular subject and a corresponding linguistic expression.

Important to Vosniadou's definition is *relationship similarity* reflected in students' use of:

◆ **Analogy:** Comparisons of two pairs that have the same relationship, as in:
  – Hot is to cold what fire is to ice
  – Desdemona is to Othello what Othello is to Iago (a victim)
◆ **Comparisons:** Statements about similarities and differences, as in:
  – I am just like Benvolio because I am often the peacekeeper when fights break out
◆ **Metaphors:** Statements in which one thing is conceived as representing another, as in:
  – All the world's a stage (*As You Like It*)
◆ **Similes:** Statements comparing two unlike things using *like* or *as*, as in:
  – She dreamt tonight she saw my statue/Which, like a fountain with a hundred spouts/Did run pure blood (*Julius Caesar*)

◆ **Allegory:** A story, picture, or play representing abstract ideas. Generally, though not always, allegories point to some religious truth or concept. Allegory is an extended metaphor in which objects, persons, and actions in a narrative (painting, text, etc.) symbolize meanings that lie outside the narrative itself. Romeo's love for Juliet, for example, could be said to have religious or spiritual dimensions evidenced in lines like, *Call me but love and I'll be new baptized.*

◆ **Parable:** A brief story with a moral or religious lesson. Parables are stories that convey essential truths about human beings and our ways. A classic example is *Aesop's Fable.* This work contains many short stories that convey moral lessons. Two famous stories include *The Hare & the Tortoise* and the *Goose with the Golden Eggs.*

Analogical reasoning examples include when students say things like:

◆ (*Henry V*): The English troops at Agincourt were like the *Little Engine that Could* – while small in number they were great in spirit.

◆ (*Henry V*): Henry's attack on the French was just like the United States' invasion of Iraq – both countries justified their reasons as noble.

◆ (*Othello*): Othello is like Speedy Gonzales – speeding forward, he sees only what is in front of him.

◆ (Acting): High volume in theater is to sound what a visual close-up is in movies – both let the audience hear and see important information.

Asking students to defend their comparisons will get them thinking, so much in fact that they could revise their comparison. If, for example, a student says, "The English troops at Agincourt were like *Dora The Explorer*", the student might be asked to think more about the comparison through high-inquiry questions like, *Why do you think so? How did you come to that conclusion? What in your reading or acting supports it? How were the troops similar to Dora?* and so on. Metaphors, similes, parables, analogies, and other comparative languages help students connect, understand, express their ideas, and demonstrate their understanding.

Wait-Time

Research has shown that it is not just the kinds of questions a teacher asks but also how much time she waits for a response that affects student learning.

"Teachers who are willing to wait recognize that inquiry thinking requires thoughtful consideration on the part of the students. Rowe points out that teachers who extend their wait-times to five seconds or longer increase 'speculative' thinking".[17]

The concept of wait-time is credited to Mary Budd Rowe, 1972.[18] She studied the length of time teachers wait between the end of the student's responses to a teacher's question and the beginning of the teacher's next question. Douglas Llewellyn summarizes Rowe's work in this area:

Rowe reports that teachers typically wait about one second following a student's answer before either repeating the answer, asking the student a follow-up question, or calling on another student. Her research indicates that when teachers practice short wait-time techniques (one second), students tend to give simple and short answers at a low-recall level. Rowe suggests that by pausing to wait three to five seconds after a student's response, desirable behaviors often result. Rowe, as well as Tobin and Capie[19] report that as the use of wait-time increases, so do:

◆ The number of student responses
◆ The number of unsolicited but appropriate responses
◆ The use of higher levels of logical thinking
◆ The incidence of speculative thinking
◆ The number of questions students ask
◆ Students supporting their answers with evidence, logic, and details
◆ Student-to-student communication and exchanges
◆ The number of positive responses
◆ The students' confidence in their ability to construct explanations

By waiting, with an uninterrupted pause for five seconds or longer, Rowe reports that the length of student responses increases by three to seven times.

Rowe[20] also reports that teachers who use longer wait-times have additional time to think about students' answers and focus more on students' responses.[21]

In addition to providing wait-time for students, Stages of Learning teaching artists often rephrased a question when blank looks appeared on students' faces after asking a question. For example, a broad question like *Why did Desdemona die?* could be clarified as *Why do you think Othello killed Desdemona instead of talking to her about his concerns?*

Setting the Stage for a Course-End Reflection

Life and learning experiences can be exhilarating, challenging, confusing, and fun. But that does not mean that the actor can make meaning of them from the experience alone. Course-end reflections help students connect the dots by providing:

- ◆ A summary of the key concepts of the course of study
- ◆ Lots of open-ended high-inquiry questions
- ◆ Time for students to respond and think
- ◆ Time for the classroom teacher and teaching artist to think in between questions
- ◆ Preparation by writing out some questions in advance

Before facilitating a full-class period of reflection with students, write on the board or on poster paper key aims for the course of study to trigger students' memories along with a couple of high-inquiry questions. Students' impressions of the experience are likely to be dominated by the culminating performance in the absence of review. Following are some suggested reflection questions.

Sample Course-End Reflection Questions

After reviewing key concepts explored during the course of study, teaching artists and classroom teachers asked students questions like (using *Othello* by way of example):

- ◆ *What did you learn from this experience? How do you know?*
- ◆ *What were some choices you made as an actor? Why did you make them?*
- ◆ *How did acting help you understand the characters in* Othello? *The plot?*
- ◆ *What is* Othello *about? What are its "big ideas" or themes? Why do you say that? What evidence can you think of to support your idea?*
- ◆ *What were you aiming to convey to the audience? Do you think the audience got it? Why or why not? How do you know? What might you do differently were you to perform the play again? What other ways might there be, other than acting, to convey these ideas?*
- ◆ *What are some benefits to working in choral character teams? How do you think it would have been different if you were to play a character alone on stage?*

◆ *What did you learn from working in a team? How do you know?*

◆ *Why did Othello kill Desdemona instead of talking to her?*

◆ *What was the main problem Othello was faced with? What ideas do you have about other ways he could have solved his problem(s)? What ending would you predict using your own ideas about what Othello should have done? Why do you think Shakespeare chose to have Othello kill Desdemona? What other artistic choices about the plot or characters do you think Shakespeare made? Why?*

◆ *Why did Iago fool Othello? Why didn't Othello see through the lies?*

◆ *Why do you think the play has lasted for hundreds of years? What is it about the play that continues to speak to people?*

◆ *How are you similar to the character you played? How are you different?*

◆ *When you reflect on your experience with acting activities and rehearsing* Othello, *what do you think you'll remember most?*

◆ *What do you see as things you'd like to learn more about* Othello, *Shakespeare, or theater?*

◆ *What did you learn about yourself during this experience? How do you know?*

◆ *What was challenging about this experience?*

◆ *What advice would you give students new to acting out Shakespeare?*

See **Instructor and Student Resources** for a certificate template to share with students after the performance or course-end reflection.

Misapplication

Questions that are closely linked to the art form, the play itself, and students' direct experience give them a stake in the experience and build understanding. Questions can be general (about acting, for example), specific (about their character in *Othello*), and dynamically linked to theater-making experience or empirical observation (in the case of assessment). Sterile disengagement of students can result when these important conditions are ignored.

High-inquiry questions, wait-time, and other points raised in this chapter may not yield deep learning connections if they are divorced from the art form in general or student experience in particular. This is true regardless of how masterful the questions are constructed or the amount of wait-time allowed. Questions must be routed in both the art-making experience (in this case theater) and the content (in this case *Othello*) with opportunities for students to inquire into what matters to them to be effective.

Notes

1 Rumohr, Floyd. "Reflection and Inquiry in Stages of Learning Practice." *Teaching Artist Journal,* 11:4, 224–233. Reprinted with permission.
2 From Schunk and Zimmerman: The term "self-regulated" refers to "learning that occurs largely from the influence of students' self-generated thoughts, feelings, strategies, and behaviors, which are oriented toward the attainment of goals" (viii).
3 Schunk, Dale H. and Barry J. Zimmerman. *Self-Regulated Learning: From Teaching to Self-Reflective Practice.* Edited by Barry J. Zimmerman and Dale H. Schunk. New York, New York: Guilford Press, 1998.
4 I do not mean to suggest that professional actors lack intellectual curiosity or that they are ignorant. I am suggesting that acting does not require of the actor knowledge or understanding beyond that required to be believable while acting the role.
5 *The Celluloid Closet.* Directed by Jeffrey Friedman Robert Epstein. Produced by Sony Pictures. 1995.
6 Pralle, Sara. "Integrating New Technology into the Methods of Education." *intime.* 2000. http://www.intime.uni.edu.
7 Donovan, S., J. Bransford, and J. Pellegrino. *How People Learn: Bridging Research and Practice.* Washington, D.C.: National Research Council, 1999.
8 Grotzer, Tina. "The Keys to Inquiry Section I: Inquiry-Learning and Learning from One's Own Experience." Project Zero Harvard Graduate School of Education. Web 12 January 2008. http://www.harvard.edu/ECT/Inquiry/inquiry1text.html.
9 Ibid.
10 Working definition of metacognition synthesized for this chapter from Hacker, Dunlosky, and Graesser (2–4, 8, 10–11, and 94) and Garcia and Pintrich (127–153).
11 Hassard, Jack. "The Art of Questioning." Minds on Science Online. Web 14 January 2008. http://scied.gsu.ed/Hassard/mos/mos.html.
12 Hassard, Jack. *The Art of Teaching Science: Inquiry and Innovation in Middle and High School.* New York, New York and Oxford, England: Oxford University Press, 2005.
13 A 4th grade student from PS 52, Staten Island, said this to me in my role as teaching artist during the 1998–99 school year.
14 The known system in this example would be mammals, which have hearts.
15 Vosniadou, Stella. "Analogical Reasoning as a Mechanism in Knowledge Acquisition: A Developmental Perspective." Technical Report No. 438. Urbana: University of Illinois Urbana-Champaign, Center for the Study of Reading. September 1988.

16 Vosniadou, Stella. 297–308.

17 Hassard, Jack. "The Art of Questioning." Minds on Science Online. Web 14 January 2008. http://scied.gsu.ed/Hassard/mos/mos.html.

18 Stahl, Robert. "Using 'Think-Time' and 'Wait-Time' Skillfully in the Classroom". *ERIC Clearinghouse for Social Studies/Social Science Education.* Web 13 January 2008.

19 Llewellyn, Douglas. *Inquire Within: Implementing Inquiry-Based Science Standards in Grades 3-8.* 2nd Edition. Thousand Oaks, California: Corwin Press, 2007.

20 Rowe, Mary Budd. "Wait-Time: Slowing Down May Be a Way of Speeding Up." *American Educator 11* (1987): 38–43, 47.

21 Llewellyn, 2007.

9

Instructor and Student Resources

Topics in each separate title below include:

- Use of Language
- Notable Quotations
- Interpreting the Play
- Cast of Characters
- Contemporary English Version (Teacher's Guide to Paraphrasing Worksheets)
- Plot Synopsis
- Acting Scripts
- Instructor and Student Resources
- Glossary

Staging Hamlet

"Something is rotten in the state of Denmark" but not for long! Hamlet will soon set things right. That is, if he doesn't spend too much time talking to the ghost of his murdered father. Some of the most famous quotations in the English language appear in *Hamlet* and they give students a lot to think about. "Brevity is the soul of wit", "To be or not to be", and "Though this be

DOI: 10.4324/9781003489733-9

madness; yet there is method in't" are just a few. Twelve characters.

- ◆ Student Paraphrasing Worksheet
- ◆ Shakespeare Certificate of Accomplishment
- ◆ Culminating Performance Program Template

> **Teaching Tip!**
>
> Don't let the number of available parts in each play dissuade you. Parts can be double cast, which means students can play multiple parts (requiring fewer students), or cast in choral character teams, which means several students speaking and moving in unison as the same character (requiring more students).

Staging Henry V

"Once more unto the breach dear friends, once more!" we hear before the great battle of Agincourt. Beware! Conspiratorial snakes are hiding in the grass waiting to strike and undermine our beloved king. Will King Henry and his "band of brothers" defeat the French in battle and assume the throne? Will he marry the French Princess? Not even a muse of fire can answer those questions. Stage it to find out! Twenty-one characters.

- ◆ Student Paraphrasing Worksheet
- ◆ Shakespeare Certificate of Accomplishment
- ◆ Culminating Performance Program Template

Staging Julius Caesar

"Beware the ides of March" warns the soothsaying Chorus in the Stage It edition of one of Shakespeare's most famous tragedies based on a historical figure (some names have been changed to protect the guilty). Power, conspiracy, and betrayal take center stage as we watch a popular politician brought down by a best friend's journey from loyal friend to savage slaughterer. "Friends, Romans, and countrymen" alike will marvel at the climax of this drama and find it hard to look away. Ten characters.

- ◆ Student Paraphrasing Worksheet
- ◆ Shakespeare Certificate of Accomplishment
- ◆ Culminating Performance Program Template

Staging Othello

A classic tale of jealousy – the green-eyed monster that devours Othello's soul! Othello, a general in the army, loves his wife, Desdemona, "not wisely, but too well". The villainous Iago manipulates Othello into believing that Desdemona has a boyfriend on the side. Othello's jealousy and mistrust lead to a tragic conclusion that reveals a terrible truth. Nine characters.

- ◆ Student Paraphrasing Worksheets
- ◆ Shakespeare Certificate of Accomplishment
- ◆ Culminating Performance Program Template

 All of the above resources are available for download on the Routledge website: www.routledge.com/9781032789149.

Glossary

Theater vocabulary and Shakespeare definitions, word usages, and pronunciations from each of *Staging Hamlet*, *Staging Henry V*, *Staging Julius Caesar*, and *Staging Othello*. See *Cast of Characters* of each play available separately for pronunciation of character names.

Pronunciation: Capital letters indicate stress. A hyphen separates the syllables.

Word and Pronunciation	Definition and Usage
Acting:	noun. Communicating an actor's interpretation of a character before an audience.
Action:	noun. Something the character does usually expressed as a verb.
Actor:	noun. A theatrical performer.
Adieu (uh-DYOO):	(*French*) interjection. Goodbye.
Agincourt (AAJ-in-kawrt):	noun. A village of northern France northwest of Arras. On October 25, 1415, Henry V of England defeated a much larger French army here. The victory showed the effectiveness of troops equipped with longbows over heavily armored knights.
Agnize (aag-NEYEZ):	verb. To acknowledge.
Aim:	noun. A description of what you want learners to know, do, and/or understand.
Alas:	An exclamation of sorrow or regret, *Ah!*
Ancient:	noun. A standard-bearer. The lowest-ranking commissioned officer.
Anon (uh-NAHN):	adverb. Presently, soon.
Archetype:	noun. A universally recognized character often described in one word. Actors often express archetype through pose.

(Continued)

Word and Pronunciation	Definition and Usage
Articulate:	verb. To pronounce words clearly (usually with staccato consonants). Articulators include: lips, teeth, tongue, and soft palate.
Askant (uh-SKAANT):	preposition. Sideways and at an angle over the water.
Assail:	verb. To attack.
Audition:	1 verb. To try out for a part. 2 noun. The act of trying out for a part.
Aught (AWT):	adverb. Anything.
Augury (AW-gyuh-ree):	noun. Predictions.
Aye (EYE):	adverb. Yes. Also *ay*.
Bade (BAAD):	verb. Past tense of *bid*.
Baron (BAA-ruhn):	noun. One of a class of tenants holding his rights and title by military or other honorable service directly from a feudal superior, such as a king.
Be't (BEET):	Contraction. Be it.
Beginning:	noun. The first part of something.
Beseech (bi-SEECH):	verb: To beg.
Blocking:	noun. Pathways and positions on the stage that ensure actors can be seen.
Bout (BOWT):	noun. A contest in a sporting event like boxing or fencing.
Brainstorm:	verb. To have a discussion that generates ideas.
Break-a-leg	verb phrase. From IdiomSite.com: "This phrase dates back to the 1920s and is superstition against wishing an actor good luck. Many people think the origin comes from when in 1865 John Wilkes Booth, who was an actor, broke his leg while leaping to kill President Lincoln during a play at the Ford's Theatre. But, this does not really seem like it is related to good luck. Some stage actors think it has to do with bending your knee when you bow, like at the end of a successful play".
Calais (kaa-LAY)	noun. A town in northern France.

(Continued)

Word and Pronunciation	Definition and Usage
Carouses (ka-ROWZ):	verb. To drink happily.
Cast:	1 verb. To assign the roles of a dramatic production to actors. 2 noun. The group of actors with specific roles.
Censure (SEHN-sher):	noun. Opinion. Today, *censure* means to criticize harshly.
Certes (SER-teez):	adverb. Certainly.
Chalice (CHAA-lis):	noun. A fancy cup used for rituals.
Character:	noun. A persona in a story. "Persona" is used because sometimes children might play animals.
Chekhov, Michael:	Famous for his acting technique, Chekhov lived from 1891 to 1955. He is remembered in Russia today as the "acting genius of the century". He acted in Hollywood movies and was nominated for an Academy Award. Chekhov's acting technique inspired the Stages of Learning practice because it focuses on character and movement, which is why it is developmentally appropriate for children ages 9-12.
Choral character teams:	noun phrase. Multiple students playing the same character.
Choral speaking:	noun. Group speaking.
Chorus (KAW-ruhs):	noun: A group of actors speaking and moving in unison.
Chide (CHEYED):	verb: To scold.
Cogging (KAHG-ing):	adjective. Fraudulent, fake.
Collaborate:	verb. To work together.
Comedy:	noun. A play that treats characters and situations in a humorous way and has a happy ending.
Communicate:	verb. To share information.
Course of study:	Several lessons exploring one idea or topic. See also "Unit of study".
Cozening (KUHZ-un-ing):	adjective. Deceiving.

(Continued)

Word and Pronunciation	Definition and Usage
Crispian (KRIS-pee-uhn):	noun. Crispinus and Crispianus, his brother, were the patron saints of shoemakers.
Crispianus (KRIS-pee-AY-nuhs):	noun. Crispinus and Crispianus, his brother, were the patron saints of shoemakers.
Crispin (KRIS-pin):	see *Crispian*.
Crusadoes (kroo-SA-dohz):	noun. Portuguese gold coins that were stamped with a cross.
Cuckold (KUK-ohld):	noun. A man whose wife has taken a boyfriend on the side.
Cue:	noun. A signal for an actor to enter a scene or to begin something.
Dally (DAA-lee):	verb. To fool with me.
Dauphin (DAW-fin)	noun. The French word for dolphin. The title was given to the French king's eldest son.
Daws (DAWZ):	noun. Stupid birds.
Designment (di-ZEYEN-muhnt):	noun: Plans.
Dialogue:	noun: Two or more actors speaking to each other.
Director:	noun. A person who is in charge of how a play is performed.
Doth (DUHTH):	verb. Do or does.
Dout (DAWT):	Contraction of *do out* meaning to extinguish.
Drama:	noun. A play (from the Greek meaning "to do" or "to act").
Ducat (DUHK-it):	noun. A coin.
Duke (DYOOK):	noun. A nobleman of the highest hereditary rank.
Dukedom (DYKOOK-duhm):	noun. The territory ruled by a duke or duchess. A duke was a nobleman of the highest hereditary rank.
Durst (DERST):	verb. Dared.
Earl (URL):	noun. A member of the British peerage, which is a system of titles of nobility in England.
Embassy (EHM-buh-see):	noun. Ambassador's message.

(Continued)

Word and Pronunciation	Definition and Usage
Emergence:	noun. Meeting standard of knowledge or skill on cue some of the time.
Emotion:	noun: Feeling. See *Feeling*.
Enow (i-NOW):	adjective. Enough.
Evidence:	noun. Visible or audible indicators that something is true or valid.
Facial Mask:	noun. Modified by an adjective: Expression of the face.
Feeling:	noun. Emotion. Researchers have identified eight basic emotions: • anger • fear • sadness • joy • disgust • anticipation • surprise • trust
Fet (FEHT):	past participle. Fetched, derived.
Fie (FEYE):	interjection. Used to express distaste.
Focus:	1 noun. Point at which the eyes are aimed. 2 verb. To focus on, pay attention to.
Foil:	noun. A blunted, rapier-like weapon used in fencing.
Gaingiving:	noun. Foreboding feeling something bad is going to happen.
Galliard (GAAL-yerd):	noun. A quick and lively dance.
Gesture:	noun. A single movement of part of the body.
God buy you:	interjection. A farewell, like *Adios*. Also *god by you*.
God-a-mercy:	interjection. God have mercy on you.
Harfleur (HAHR-fler):	noun. A town in France on the north bank of the mouth of the Seine river.
Hark:	verb. A call to urge or start something.

(Continued)

Word and Pronunciation	Definition and Usage
Hath (HATH):	verb. Has, have, or had.
Hebenon (HEHB-uh-non):	noun. A poison.
Heir (AIR):	noun. Person who will inherit.
Hence (HENS):	adverb. Therefore. From this time; for this reason.
Hies (HIZE):	verb. To hurry onward.
Hither (HITH-er):	adverb. Toward this way.
House:	noun. The place where the audience sits.
Husbandry:	noun. Thrift.
Imagine:	verb. To see a mental image or picture of something.
Import:	verb. Means. To be of importance.
Improvisation:	noun. Acting without a script.
Improvise:	verb. To create with little or no preparation.
In't (INT):	Contraction of *in it*.
Inquire:	verb. To ask questions that enable the learner to understand something.
Instruments (of the actor):	plural noun. The voice and body. See also "tools of the actor".
Intention:	noun. A character's want (sometimes called "motivation").
Interpret:	verb. To perform in a way that conveys understanding of the actor's ideas and decisions about a character.
Knave (NAYV):	noun. Villain.
Knight:	noun. A military man in honorable service to a nobleman.
Legato:	adverb and adjective. Smooth, quick or slow (in tempo) movement and speech. Legato is not a total opposite of staccato because legato can be rapid or slow. Staccato is always rapid.
Level:	noun. Position on a scale (i.e., high, medium, or low).
Liege (LEEJ):	noun: Sovereign lord, superior to the person speaking.

(Continued)

Word and Pronunciation	Definition and Usage
Lines:	noun. Text spoken by an actor.
List:	verb. To listen.
Lord:	noun. A word used to describe any of the titled men of Britain such as a Duke or Earl.
Majesty	noun. A king or queen.
Mastery:	noun. Meeting standard of knowledge or skill on cue all of the time.
Masham (MAA-suhm)	noun. A region in North Yorkshire, England.
Matin (MAA-tin):	noun. Morning.
Mazard (MAAZ-erd):	noun, (slang). Head.
Methinks:	verb phrase. It seems to me.
Monologue:	noun. Text intended to be spoken by one character.
Moor (MOOR):	noun. A member of the Muslim people of northwest Africa.
Mountebank (MOUN-tuh-baangk):	noun. A quack, charlatan, pretender. In *Hamlet*, the king obtains an oil or ointment from a mountebank, meaning that it is poisonous.
Naught (NAWT):	adjective. Worthless, useless.
Nay (NAY):	adverb. No.
Ne'r (NAIR):	Contraction for *never*.
Neutral position:	adjective modifying a noun. Physical state of readiness to receive instruction or direction. The visible behavior of readiness: two feet flat on the floor, arms down at the side, belly deep and wide, silent, and focused. See also *Ready position*.
Off-Book:	Lines have been memorized.
Oft (AWFT):	adverb: Often.
On-Book:	Lines have not been memorized. The actor still needs script ("book") in hand during rehearsals.
Pathway:	noun. A course of movement.
Perchance (PER-chantz):	adverb. By chance.
Perdition (per-DISH-uhn):	noun. Complete destruction.

(Continued)

Word and Pronunciation	Definition and Usage
Petard (pi-TAHRD):	noun: A small bomb used to blow up gates and walls.
Playwright:	noun. A person who writes a play.
Plot:	noun. Story line. The sequence of actions in a whole play.
Pose:	1 noun. A still shape of the body. 2 verb. To assume a shape of the body.
Posy:	1 noun. A small inscription on the inside of a ring. 2 A small bunch of flowers.
Prithee:	interjection. Pray you, please.
Process:	noun. A series of actions or steps toward achieving an end.
Producer:	noun. A person responsible for all business aspects of putting on a play like paying the actors and staff.
Proficiency:	noun. Meeting standard of knowledge or skill on cue most of the time.
Prologue:	noun. An introduction. The actor speaking the prologue in Shakespeare's plays often wore a long black velvet cloak.
Puissant (PYOO-suhnt):	adjective. Strong, powerful.
Radiate:	noun. To send out a feeling through the face or voice.
Rapier (RAYP-yer):	noun: A long, straight sword.
Ready position:	adjective modifying a noun. Physical state of readiness to receive instruction or direction. The visible behavior of readiness: two feet flat on the floor, arms down at the side, belly deep and wide, silent, and focused. See also *Neutral position*.
Reflect:	verb. To think deeply or carefully about something you have done.
Rehearse:	verb. Practice.
Rheum (ROOM):	noun. Mucus.
Role:	noun. The character or part played by an actor. The word derives from when actors' lines were written on *rolls* of paper.

(Continued)

Word and Pronunciation	Definition and Usage
Scene:	noun. A place or setting where an action occurs.
Script:	noun. The written text spoken by an actor.
Sequence:	1 noun. An order in which things follow each other. 2 verb. To arrange in an order.
Sir (SUHR):	noun. A man of rank or position. Used as a title before the given name of a baron, baronet, or knight. A man who has completed service as a page and squire.
Skill:	noun. Ability (to do something).
Slubber:	verb. To defile, soil, or stain.
Soliloquy (Soh-LIL-a-kwee):	noun. Talking alone on stage.
Sovereign (SAHV-uh-rin):	adjective. Supreme.
Space:	noun. Area. General space: adjective modifying a noun. Area that is occupied by several people. Personal space: adjective modifying a noun. Area that you occupy. *Special thanks to teaching artist Margot Fought for her assistance with this definition.*
Speech:	noun. Sound produced from speaking (primarily consonants). See also *voice* and *articulate*.
Squire (SKWEYER):	noun. A youth being trained for knighthood.
Staccato:	adverb and adjective. Sharp, quick movement and speech. Staccato is not a total opposite of legato because staccato is always rapid. Legato can be rapid or slow.
Stage combat:	noun/verb term: Movements that create the illusion of physical fighting without causing harm to anyone.
Stage directions:	Sections of the stage where actors move and stand.
Stoup (STOOP):	noun. A large drinking vessel (approximately two liters).
Strategy:	noun. A plan (designed to achieve an aim).

(Continued)

Word and Pronunciation	Definition and Usage
Strumpet (STRUHM-pit):	noun. A low person.
Synopsis:	noun. A brief summary.
Tableau Vivant:	noun phrase (plural: tableaux vivant). A frozen moment presented on stage by actors who remain silent and motionless as if in a picture. (French: tableau: picture + vivant: living).
Tarry (TAHR-ee):	verb. Stay, wait.
Tempest:	noun. A violent storm.
Tempo:	noun. Speed of something.
Tenders:	noun. Declaration or offer.
Theater (also Theatre):	noun. The production of a play. American spelling: theater British spelling: theatre
Theatrical:	noun. Generally exaggerated and suitable for a performance before an audience.
Thee (THEE):	pronoun. You.
Theme:	noun. What the play means (not what happens).
Thence (THEHNS):	adverb: Away.
Thine (THEYEN):	possessive pronoun. Yours or your.
Thither (THI-ther):	adverb. To or toward that place.
Thou (THOW):	familiar pronoun. You.
Thus:	adverb. So, therefore.
Thy (THEYE):	possessive pronoun. Your.
'Tis (TIZ):	Contraction for *it is*.
'Twas (TWAZ):	Contraction for *it was*.
Tools of the Actor:	phrase. Physical objects used by professional actors, such as scripts, props, and pencils.
Tragedy:	noun. A play that treats characters and situations as sad, and the main character suffers.
Transition:	noun. The process of changing from one state or condition to another.

(Continued)

Word and Pronunciation	Definition and Usage
Twiggen (TWIG-uhn):	adjective. Having a wicker covering.
Unit of study:	Several lessons exploring one idea or topic. See also *Course of study*.
Unto (UHN-too):	preposition. In addition to, in relation or regard to, according to, of, against.
Usurp (yoo-ZERP):	verb. To take possession of.
Verb:	noun. An action word.
Voice:	noun. Sound produced from speaking.
Volume:	noun. Level of loudness.
Vouchsafe (vowch-SAYF):	verb. To allow.
Wanton (WAHN-tuhn):	noun. A fool.
Wherefore (HWAIR-fore):	adverb. Why.
Wherein (HWAIR-in):	adverb. In what, in that, in which, in whatever.
Wings:	noun. The off-stage area to the right and left used as entrances and exits.
Withal (with-AWL):	adverb. With this. With it.
You:	formal pronoun. You.
Zounds (ZOONDZ):	Interjection, a corruption of *god's wounds*, pronounced *zoondz*: used to express surprise, anger, or indignation.

References

Americans for the Arts Research Reports Arts Education. https://www. americansforthearts.org/by-program/reports-and-data/research-studies-publications/americans-for-the-arts-publications/research-reports#education. February 20, 2024.

Applewhite, Ashton, William R. Evans III, and Andrew Frothingham. *And I Quote: The Definitive Collection of Quotes, Sayings, and Jokes for the Contemporary Speechmaker*. New York, New York: St. Martin's Press, 2003.

Arts in Schools Report 2020–2021. NYC Department of Education. P11, 15.

Basil, John and Stephanie Gunning. *Will Power: How to Act Shakespeare in 21 Days*. New York, New York: Applause Theatre Book, 2006.

Branagh, Kenneth. *Hamlet*. New York, New York: W.W. Norton & Company, 1996.

Brownell, Ginanne. "The Mind-Expanding Value of Arts Education". *New York Times*. May 2, 2023.

Bransford, John, Suzanne Donovan, and James Pellegrino. *How People Learn: Bridging Research and Practice*. Washington, D.C.: National Research Council (U.S.) Committee on Learning Research and Educational Practice, 1999.

Collaborative Classroom. Caring School Community K-8. Retrieved online March 22, 2024. https://info.collaborativeclassroom.org/caring-school-community-k-8?utm_term=casel%20framework&utm_campaign=CSC+-+National&utm_source=adwords&utm_medium=ppc&hsa_acc=9861834821&hsa_cam=12966904783&hsa_grp=124796945474&hsa_ad=519116708557&hsa_src=g&hsa_tgt=kwd-1027273283237&hsa_kw=casel%20framework&hsa_mt=b&hsa_net=adwords&hsa_ver=3&gad_source=1&gclid=Cj0KCQjw2PSvBhD-jARIsAKc2cgNSw1IhkbZC2l7mGI1i8qm6oyFn7P0t1hPM7Pq2Jxzq5d-9MaKLucO8aAhXdEALw_wcB.

Colman, A. *A Dictionary of Psychology*. 3rd Edition. Oxford, UK: Oxford University Press, 2008.

Crowe, Patty. *Quotes on Art and Artists: Mankind's Wisdom on Art from Plato to Picasso*. Edited by Laura Wertz. Arlington, Virginia: Richer Resources Publications, 2006.

Dekker, Thomas, Henry Chettle, and William Haughton. *Patient Grissil: A Comedy*. London: The Shakespeare Society, 1841.

Donovan S., J. Bransford, and J. Pellegrino. *How People Learn: Bridging Research and Practice*. Washington, D.C.: National Research Council, 1999.

Douglas J. Hacker, John Dunlosky, and Arthur C. Graesser. *Metacognition in Educational Theory and Practice.* Mahwah and London: Lawrence Erlbaum Associates, 1998.

Doyle, John and Ray Lischner. *Shakespeare for Dummies.* New York, New York: Dummies Press, 1999.

Ewell, Peter T. "Organizing for Learning: A Point of Entry." *intime.* 1997. Web 12 November 2012. http://www.intime.uni.edu/model/learning/learn_summary.html.

Garcia, Teresa and P.R. Pintrich. "Regulating motivation and cognition in the classroom: The role of self-schemas and self-regulatory strategies." In *Self-Regulation of Learning and Performance: Issues and Educational Applications*, by B.J. Zimmerman and D.H. Schunk. Hillsdale, New Jersey: Lawrence Erlbaum Associates, 1994.

Gardner, Howard. *The Theory of Multiple Intelligences.* New York, New York: Basic Books, 1993.

Giovanelli, Alison, Christina F. Mondi, and Arthur Reynolds. "Fostering Socio-emotional Learning through Early Childhood Intervention". *International Journal of Child Care and Education Policy.* 15, Article Number 6 (2021).

González, Félix Rodríguez. *Spanish Loanwords in the English Language: A Tendency Towards Hegemony Reversal.* Berlin and New York: Mouten de Gruyter, 1996.

Goswami, Usha. *Analogical Reasoning in Children.* Hillsdale, England: Lawrence Erlbaum Associates, 1992.

Grotzer, Tina. "The Keys to Inquiry Section I: Inquiry-Learning and Learning from One's Own Experience." Project Zero Harvard Graduate School of Education. Web 12 January 2008. http://www.harvard.edu/ECT/Inquiry/inquiry1text.html.

Hassard, Jack. *The Art of Teaching Science: Inquiry and Innovation in Middle and High School.* New York, New York and Oxford, England: Oxford University Press, 2005.

Hassard, Jack. "The Art of Questioning." Minds on Science Online. Web 14 January 2008. http://scied.gsu.ed/Hassard/mos/mos.html.

Honan, Park. *Shakespeare: A Life.* New York, New York: Oxford University Press, 1998.

Houghton Mifflin Company. *The Houghton Mifflin Dictionary of Biography.* Edited by Joseph Pickett. Boston, Massachusetts: Houghton Mifflin Company, 2003.

Jenkins, James. *Descriptive Language Terms.* Spring 2006. http://www.mtsac.edu/~jjenkins/desc.html (accessed January 8, 2013).

Jones, Beau Fly, and Lorna Idol. *Dimensions of Thinking and Cognitive Instruction.* Hillsdale, New Jersey: Lawrence Erlbaum Associates, 1990.

Jones, Stephanie M., Katharine E. Brush, Samantha Wettje, Thelma Ramirez, Aashna Poddar, Alisha Kannarr, Sophie P. Barnes, Annie Hooper, Gretchen Brion-Meisels, and Edwin Chng. "Navigating SEL From the Inside Out". Wallace Foundation. November 2022.

LaMar, Virginia and Louis B. Wright. *Hamlet*. Washington D.C.: Folger Library General Reader's Shakespeare, 1958.

Llewellyn, Douglas. *Inquire Within: Implementing Inquiry-Based Science Standards in Grades 3-8*. 2nd Edition. Thousand Oaks, California: Corwin Press, 2007.

Luvmour, Ba. *Nurturing a Child's Consciousness: Natural Learning Relationships and the Roles of Parents, Educators and Caregivers*. Independently Published, 2022.

Luvmour, Josette. *Grow Together: Parenting as a Path to Well-being, Wisdom, and Joy*. N. Charleston, South Carolina: Create Space Publishing, 2017.

Macrone, Michael. *Brush Up Your Shakespeare!* New York, New York: Gramercy Books, 1998.

Manning, Brenda H. *Cognitive Self-Instruction for Classroom Processes*. Albany: State University of New York Press, Albany, 1991.

McQuain, Jeffrey and Stanley Malles. *Coined by Shakespeare: Words and Meanings First Penned by the Bard*. Springfield, Massachusetts: Merriam-Webster, 1998.

Moston, Doug. *The First Folio of Shakespeare 1623*. New York, New York: Applause Books, 1995.

New York City Department of Education. *Blueprint for Teaching and Learning in the Arts: Theater: Grades PreK-12*. New York, New York: NYC Department of Education, 2005, 82–85.

Perfect, Timothy J. and Bennett L. Schwartz, eds. *Applied Metacognition*. Cambridge, New York, Melbourne, Madrid, and Cape Town: Cambridge University Press, 2002.

Plutchik, Robert. Sixseconds "Plutchik's Wheel of Emotions: Exploring the Emotion Wheel". Web 29 December 2023. https://www.6seconds.org/2022/03/13/plutchik-wheel-emotions/.

Plutchik, Robert. Corroborated and clarified during a phone conversation with Mrs. Plutchik in 2008.

Pralle, Sara. "Integrating New Technology into the Methods of Education." *intime*. 2000. http://www.intime.uni.edu.

Quennell, Peter and Hamish Johnson. *Who's Who in Shakespeare*. New York, New York: Routledge, 2002.

Rees, Nigel. *Brewer's Famous Quotations: 5000 Quotations and the Stories Behind Them*. London: Sterling Publishing Company, 2006.

Rowe, Mary Budd. "Wait-Time: Slowing Down May Be a Way of Speeding Up." *American Educator* 11, (1987): 38–43, 47.

Rozakis, Laurie. *The Complete Idiot's Guide to Shakespeare*. New York, New York: Alpha Books, 1999.

Rumohr, Floyd. "Michael Chekhov, Psychological Gesture, and the Thinking Heart." *Movement for Actors*, by Nicole Potter. Edited by Nicole Potter. New York, New York: Allworth Press, 2002.

Rumohr, Floyd. "Reflection and Inquiry in Stages of Learning Practice." *Teaching Artist Journal*, 11, no. 4: 224–233. This was published online Sep 25 2013. More info: https://www.tandfonline.com/doi/abs/10.1080/15411796.2013.815544

Scheeder, Louis and Shane Ann Younts. *All the Words on Stage*. Hanover, New Hampshire: Smith and Krause, 2002.

Schunk, Dale H. and Barry J. Zimmerman. *Self-Regulated Learning: From Teaching to Self-Reflective Practice*. Edited by Barry J. Zimmerman and Dale H. Schunk. New York, New York: Guilford Press, 1998.

Spolin, Viola. *Theater Games for Rehearsal: A Director's Handbook*. Evanston, Illinois: Northwestern University Press, 2010.

Spolin, Viola. *Theater Games for the Classroom: A Teacher's Handbook*. Evanston, Illinois: Northwestern University Press, 1986.

Stages of Learning. "Lexicon of Terms." Brooklyn, New York: Unpublished, 1994–2008.

Stahl, Robert. "Using 'Think-Time' and 'Wait-Time' Skillfully in the Classroom". *ERIC Clearinghouse for Social Studies/Social Science Education*. Web 13 January 2008.

The Celluloid Closet. Directed by Jeffrey Friedman Robert Epstein. Produced by Sony Pictures. 1995.

Tucker, Patrick. *Secrets of Acting Shakespeare: The Original Approach*. New York, New York: Routledge Theatre Arts Books, 2002.

Vosniadou, Stella and Andrew Ortony. "Analogical Reasoning as a Mechanism in Knowledge Acquisition: A Developmental Perspective." Technical Report No. 438. Urbana: University of Illinois Urbana-Champaign, Center for the Study of Reading. September 1988.

Vosniadou, Stella and Andrew Ortony. "Analogical Reasoning in Cognitive Development." *Metaphor and Symbol*, 10, no. 4 (1995): 297–308.

Vosniadou, Stella and Andrew Ortony. "Re: Similarity and Analogical Reasoning." Message to the author. 16 January 2008. E-mail.

Vosniadou, Stella and Andrew Ortony. *Similiarity and Analogical Reasoning*. Cambridge, New York, Melbourne: Cambridge University Press, 1989.

Walter, J.H. *King Henry V Arden Shakespeare*. New York and London: Routledge, 1990.

Wood, Chip. *Yardsticks: Children in the Classroom Ages 4–14*. 3rd Edition. Turner Falls, Massachusetts: Northeast Foundation for Children, 2007.

Younts, Louis Scheeder and Shane Ann. *All the Words on Stage*. Hanover: Smith and Krause, 2002.